Endorsements

Rhema is truly living out his name and always baffles one with his insights from the word of God. *A Suspect for Success* lifts the heart with great insights and nuggets of truth. It is written to bring out the best of God from everyone no matter how low the person is. I am very proud of my beloved son and pleased to recommend this book to you.

Dr. Jude Ehiemere
Author, 'Tselem: The Image God made'
Chief Medical Director, Living Word Mission Hospitals
Vice President, Living Word Ministries Inc.

In my 50 years of ministry, this is one of the most powerful books I have read. I have seen many people abandon their God given destinies because they misinterpreted the purpose of disappointments. Thanks Rhema for your God-given insight and reminder that the only time we don't face opposition is if we are not in the game of life.

Rev. Ronald E. Fraker
Senior Pastor, Victory Chapel,
Church of the Foursquare Gospel,
Arcadia, California.

I encourage you to read this book and be blessed. I have known Rhema for over two decades and he is definitely a blessing to this generation.

Apostle Emma Okorie
Author, 'Marriage Without Tears'
President, Living Word Ministries Inc. & Founder, Rhema University Nigeria

A Suspect for Success is an insightful translation of the truth, revealing the power to set men free. I have read this book and recommend it.

Pst. Steve Austin
Senior Pastor, Champions Community Church,
Houston, Texas.

God is proud of this book. The wisdom expressed on the pages of this book is remarkable. It will become your source of inspiration to build your dreams. It will become your instruction manual to overcome adversity. This book is a "must-have" in every believer's library.

Nurisha Liggins
Author, 'Living the Light' 90 day devotional
Administrator, Mike Murdock Ministries & The Wisdom Center,
Ft. Worth, Texas.

A *Suspect for Success* is an encouraging and uplifting reminder that God is ultimately in control and that He works all things together for our good regardless of the schemes of the adversary. I highly recommend it.

Pst. Rick Minett
Senior Pastor, Grace Community Church,
Houston, Texas.

If you have a dream in your heart you wish to accomplish, this book is a must for you! A *Suspect for Success* is full of thought provoking revelations and divine insights with inspiring perspectives for everyone. It sure will explode in every dreamer's heart. In writing this book, Rhema is not just a prime suspect for success, he is the chief target.

Simisola Komolafe
TV Host and Associate Producer
Turning Point International, Christian Broadcasting Network (CBN),
Virginia Beach, Virginia.

This is definitely a masterpiece. The depth of spiritual insight and practical principles embedded in this book is unarguably outstanding.

Psts. Ikoro & Ndudi Chukwu
Presidents, Mission Africa
Senior Pastors, Living Word Ministries
Seattle, Washington.

This book is a must-read, if you've ever known the struggles of leading a church, business, team or family.

Pst. Chase Austin
Lead Pastor, Champions Community Church
Houston, Texas.

Often times, great men are thought to have assumed their prominence with little effort. However the reality is that great men are born out of great trials. *A Suspect for Success* is an undulating current of hope for those who had previously despised their secret preparation. I recommend this to anyone who has felt that nagging pang to be more!

Dr. & Dr. (Mrs) Victor Ehiemere
Principal Life Coach, Strategic Leadership and Foresight Consultants
EXCEL today Resources.

Undoubtedly, one of the best books I have read in recent times. This is a timeless piece. It is a dreamer's companion, a manager's template, a student's teacher and a must for every Library. It challenges the mind, stirs the Spirit and re-invigorates the Body. If you are desirous of making supernatural strides, this dynamite captures it all.

Pst. Jerry Eze
Author, 'Streams of Joy Devotional'
President, Streams of Joy International Ministries.

I highly recommend *A Suspect for Success* and know it will surely bless you. Rhema carries an unusual grace for divine transformation.

Pst. Abimbola Komolafe
Senior Pastor, Jubilee Church, RCCG
Manchester, United Kingdom.

Rhema just has a way with words as his name goes. *A Suspect for Success* is a motivational masterpiece and a handbook for success.

Pst. Chinedu Udonsi
Author, Developing a Kingdom Mentality
Senior Pastor, Joy of The Nations Christian Center,
London, United Kingdom.

*20% of proceeds from this book go into missions, charities and non-profit organizations that are partnered with,
More Information on page 100.*

A
SUSPECT FOR SUCCESS

Setback for a season, Setup for a reason

RHEMA EHIEMERE

Global Relevance Enterprises

A SUSPECT FOR SUCCESS: SETBACK FOR A SEASON, SETUP FOR A REASON

Copyright © 2012 Rhema Ehiemere

Published by Global Relevance Enterprises

All rights reserved. No part of this book maybe reproduced in any form, stored in a retrieval system, or transmitted in any form by any means-electronic, mechanical, phototocopy, recording or otherwise, without the prior written permission of the publisher.

Unless otherwise indicated, all Scripture quotations are taken from the KING JAMES VERSION, Authorized King James Version.
Other Scripture quotations are taken from the following sources:
CEV- Contemporary English Version®.
Copyright © 1995 American Bible Society. All rights reserved.
ESV- English Standard Version®. Copyright© 2001 by Crossway Bibles, a ministry of the Good News Publishers of Wheaton, IL.
GNT- Good News Translation® (Today's English Version, Second Edition)
Copyright © 1992 American Bible Society. All rights reserved.
GW- Scripture is taken from GOD'S WORD®, © 1995 God's Word to the Nations. Used by permission of Baker Publishing Group.
MSG- Scripture taken from The Message. Copyright ©1993, 1994, 1995, 1996, 2000, 2001, 2002. Used by permission of NavPress Publishing Group.
NCV- Scripture taken from the New Century Version. Copyright © 2005 by Thomas Nelson Inc. Used by permission. All rights reserved.
NLT- Scripture quotations are taken from the Holy Bible, New Living Translation, copyright ©1996, 2004, 2007 by Tyndale House Foundation. Used by permission of Tyndale House Publishers, Inc., Carol Stream, Illinois 60188. All rights reserved.
Websters- Noah Webster's Version. ©1833 New Haven: Durrie and Peck. Reprinted 1987 Grand Rapids: Baker Book House.

Printed in the USA
Cover Design by Palette Ink©
ISBN-13: 978-0-615-60203-5

Dedication

To God Almighty for His Grace. Thank you for loving, calling, anointing and appointing me for this high calling, despite my faults and frailties.

To my help meet, beautiful wife and best friend, Nkiruka Stephanie; you are the paragon of exquisiteness, the complete quintessence of feminine pulchritude and the potpourri of life's choicest flavors. You will always be my baby and lady. I love you mama.

To everyone who believes the future is bigger, better and brighter despite the storms and setbacks they face presently.

Acknowledgements

I'm forever grateful to God for the Grace and insights he gave me to write this book.

To my first ministry, my one and only wife, Nkiruka Stephanie; thank you for believing in me, standing by me and praying for me. I appreciate the efforts you put to make this book a reality. You are a virtuous wife indeed.

I want to appreciate my parents, Dr. Jude and Esther Ehiemere. Thanks for training me up in the way I should go. Your sacrifice of love and discipline has made me what I am today. To my parents-in-law, Dr. Linus and Mareen Ojukwu, Thanks for your love, encouragements and prayers. I love you all dearly.

To my siblings, Dr. Victor, Dr. Amblessed, Uzoma Zoe, Randy, Sando, Victor and Paul, thank you so much for being there for me. You all have been dependable and reliable like marble pillars set upon sockets of gold. I love you to my marrows.

A big thank you to Apostle Emma & Chi Okorie. Your prayers and advice have given my speed amongst my peers. I am a proof that God sent you with an apostolic mandate.

Thanks Pst. & Mrs. Okey Nwagu for your unconditional love and support. You are real pastors indeed. I'm grateful to Pst. & Pst. (Mrs.) Abimbola and Folu Komolafe. Thanks for your prophecies. Words are not enough to express my heartfelt gratitude for all you've done for me. Thanks Pastors Steve, Cyndi and Chase, your humility and consistency is amazing. Thank you for being a blessing.

Many thanks to all the pastors and members of the Living Word Ministries World Wide, Jubilee Church(RCCG), Manchester and

Champions Community Church, Houston. You all are the greatest family in the world.

Special thanks to Pst. & Mrs. Ron and Sandy Fraker, Rev. & Mrs. Henry and Favor Emmanuel, Rev. Charles Dorsey, Pst. Rick Minett, Nurisha Liggins, Pst. Chinedu Udonsi, Simisola Komolafe, Pst. KayCee, Pst. Jerry Eze, Pst. & Mrs Ikoro and Ndudi Chukwu. You have made all the difference in my life and you hold a very special place in my heart. Thanks for all your help.

To all the Staff of Pallete Ink, I have often wondered how you concretized the abstract of my mind. You did a great job.

To everyone that has contributed to make this work possible, thank you and God bless you richly.

CONTENTS

Introduction ... 1

1: You're alive because you've not yet arrived ... 5

2: Any vision without an opposition is an illusion in disguise ... 15

3: Never apologize for what God wants you to celebrate over ... 23

4: The past has passed; your future is not in what you lost, it's in who you are ... 31

5: Treasure your trials; hurtful situations often birth helpful connections ... 39

6: Your real measure is revealed under pressure ... 47

7: Isolation is not rejection, but preparation for promotion ... 53

8: Situations are meant to refine you, not define you ... 61

9: Great people are real people; they never hide their true personality behind their positions ... 73

10: The manifestation of your dreams begins with the interpretation of the dreams of others ... 81

11: It's comeback time; your setback can not stop your set time ... 87

Get connected ... 98

Selected References ... 101

INTRODUCTION

It was the blooming spring of 2011 in the United Kingdom. My wife and I were watching an exciting soccer game between Manchester United and Arsenal in the famous Old Trafford Stadium. As the game progressed, I spotted an Arsenal striker. Even though he did not have the ball, he was still being marked closely by a Manchester United defender. After the match, that picture flashed through my mind again and for some reason I just kept thinking about it all the way home.

Usually when this happens to me, I know God is trying to tell me something. Suddenly, it dawned on me that although the striker was not in possession of the ball, the defender knew that he (the striker) was still a threat. The mere fact that he was still on the field meant the ball could be passed to him and with only few seconds left to the end of the game he could score the winning goal. Thus, even though everybody's attention was not on him at the moment, the defender was very alert and ready to challenge him once the ball got to him.

Life is very much like a soccer game. Those who are suspects for success may not have all the attention now because they do not have the ball. They may not have the right background, education or connections. In fact, they may be going through the worst season of their life at the moment. They may be facing debilitating setbacks and challenges they have no control over.

Yet, they are still a source of concern and threat to the enemy. He knows that as long as they are in the game, remain focused and stay in their positions, they can get the ball and score a goal at anytime.

Introduction

This is why the enemy does not only attack those in the spotlight with all the attention but also those who are in position and have the potential to change the outcome of the game. You may not have all the attention now but you are still in the game of life and a threat to the enemy. He can sense the potential for greatness and the prospect of success within you. The predetermined power of purpose and irresistible force of destiny within you scares him. That is why he marks, tackles, attacks and challenges you.

Oftentimes, challenges also come through people who have a preview of our future and want to abort our destiny. Out of envy and jealousy for Joseph's dream his brothers tired to kill him. They were after what he will become not who he was already. No wonder they said:

> '... Look, here comes the <u>hero of those dreams! Let's kill him</u> and throw him into a pit... <u>Then we'll see what happens to those dreams.</u>'
>
> **Genesis 37: 19-20 (CEV)**

Success can be sensed long before it even manifests. It's amazing how the inherent greatness within people can be perceived in its latent state before it materializes. Often times, the enemy picks up these signals of success afar off and tries to use negative people or adverse situations to stop, stifle and suffocate these embryonic dream seeds. But the force of destiny is already predetermined and unstoppable.

All through the Bible, we see this pattern repeated. The enemy wanted to use Pharaoh to kill all male Israelite babies because he wanted to destroy Moses, who was destined to liberate Israel. Joseph's brothers tried to kill him because of his dream. Saul tried to kill David when he sensed that he was going to be king. Herod tried to kill all the

Introduction

male babies because he wanted to get rid of Jesus. The enemy is and has always been after the destiny of great people.

I wrote this book because many great people have aborted their great destinies because they have buckled under the weight of life's pressure. Friends, Godly dreams always attract envy, criticism and opposition. We don't always go through situations because something is wrong with us, but because something is right with us. Sometimes, the enemy attacks us presently just because of our potentials.

This book is a compilation of practical lessons and powerful principles extracted from the life of Joseph, our main character. We glean a lot from his experiences that serve as a template for understanding the tumultuous terrain of life's seasons. We learn the right attitude we must have as we carry our dream through its trimesters. We understand the perils of greatness and finally we discover how and why we need to trust God till he makes our dreams dawn.

I invite you to take this journey with me as we promenade through the matrix of Joseph's life. All the attention may not be on you now, but the enemy is still marking you closely because he knows you are a suspect for success. Eventually, you will realize that all you went through was all a setup for a divine reason.

Rhema Ehiemere
Houston, Texas.

Introduction

1
YOU'RE ALIVE BECAUSE YOU'VE NOT YET ARRIVED

God does not give us dreams because they are sensible but because they are possible. There is always a tendency to rationalize or doubt the certainty of our dreams, when we find ourselves passing through difficult situations that contradict the possibility of their occurrence.

However, challenges are not always a sign of negative decisions made in the past. They may be positive indicators of greatness in the future. Sometimes the issues we face in life are divine pointers from God signaling that we are at the verge of a major breakthrough. They may be disguised as problems because the enemy is only after those with potentials for greatness. However in reality, these setbacks are signposts of opportunities that herald a new season in our lives.

Our lives were concluded in God before we were created. Therefore, human reasoning, personal excuses and public opinion are already too late to become the determinants of our destiny. God's purpose will always come to pass even if the odds are stacked against you. This is why Godly dreams do not always make sense to the natural mind. It always defies man-made rules, reasoning and rationale. Besides, we must never forget that these dreams originate from the Almighty God whom our minds cannot even fully grasp and comprehend.

When we are impregnated with a dream, it is an opportunity to experience and express only an infinitesimal aspect of God's unfathomable greatness. It is not a season to focus on our weakness, doubt our dreams or abort our future because of the pressure of life's vicissitudes.

There will be times when we will encounter the prenatal seasons of irritations and painful contractions of giving birth to our dreams. Nonetheless, we must not focus on the present pain, but on the imminent joy of delivery. This is the time to conceive the invisible, believe the impossible and receive strength to do the incredible.

God does not play games when it comes to issues about our future. If He put a dream in your spirit, no matter how mind-blowing and overwhelming it may seem, He'll keep you alive to see it come to pass. If you are still alive, then what He showed you has not come to pass yet. There is still more ahead, today may appear bleak, but the future is still bright.

Right now, the chances of your dream materializing may appear slim because of what you are going through, but I have good news for you. Your best days are still ahead. You have not arrived there yet. You have not accomplished everything yet. There is no need to give up so soon. This is not just a cliché or motivational quote. This is God's word over your life and it must complete the assignment it was given. The fulfillment of your destiny is tied to the word of God. The bible says;

'So will the <u>words out of my mouth</u> not come back empty handed. <u>They do the work</u> I sent them to do, <u>they'll complete the assignment</u> I gave them.'

Isaiah 55:11 (MSG)

THE NEXT LEVEL IS ACCESSIBLE

In a quantum physics class I took in high school, I was taught about a famous Danish physicist, Neils Bohr. He propounded that when atoms are excited, by absorbing energy during heating or by collision with a fast moving electron, they jump to higher energy levels. However, if they are left undisturbed, they drop to the lowest available energy level which is their ground state.[1]

Recently, I thought about this. It occurred to me that it was actually the heat and increase in temperature that provided the right environment to move the atoms to higher energy levels. The atoms never moved to the next energy level till they were excited.

Similarly in life, we find ourselves in heated situations and circumstances, in which we seemingly have no control over. But we must take our eyes off the thermometer and realize that God is in control of the thermostat. He regulates the temperature and would not give us more than we can bear. He would only permit enough heat just to move us to higher levels in life.

Most times what we call affliction is simply God's preparation for our promotion. Many of us desire to enter into the next level in our career, ministry and business. But we do not want to experience the heat that *excites* us to the next level. Job went through a lot of crises in the Bible. But he realized that his next level was accessible through the process. He knew his steps were still ordered by God. In the midst of afflictions, he was certain God was preparing him for a greater future. No wonder he said:

> *'But he knows the way that I take; <u>when he has tried me, I shall come out as gold.</u>'*
>
> **Job 23: 10 (ESV)**

YOUR STEPS ARE STILL ORDERED

Often times we love to quote the scripture in Psalm 37:23 that says, *'The steps of the righteous man are ordered by the Lord…'* However, when we pass through tough times we fail to realize that our steps are *still* ordered and we are still part of God's plan. As thoughts of defeat and disappointment flash through our minds, we tend to conclude that our future is going to be a clone of our present circumstance. We feel like God is through with us. This feeling often blinds us to the realities of life, driving us to make permanent decisions based on temporary situations. But even in the worst situations, God assures us that our steps are ordered and He will move us to higher levels in time.

Consider Joseph in the book of Genesis 37. God gave him a dream of greatness at the age of 17. But he had to go through an unconventional path to get to the Palace. Nevertheless, on his way to the pit, his steps were still ordered. When he was falsely accused by Portiphar's wife, his steps were still ordered. When he was dumped in the prison, his steps were still ordered. When the Chief Butler forgot him in prison immediately after his release, his steps were still ordered.

Everything he went through was part of God's *heated* plan to move him to a higher level, the palace. Just like Joseph, whatever we go through is not a surprise to God; it's part of the puzzle in His big picture. If He permitted it, then it has a purpose; maybe not now, but in the future when it all comes together. God is a master strategist. He knows how to use the things that were meant to upset us, to set us up. He used the fire that was meant to burn up the three Hebrew children to move them into positions of prominence (Daniel 3). No wonder God says;

'I know what I'm doing. I have it all planned out-plans to take care of you, not abandon you, plans to give you the future you hope for…'

Jeremiah 29:11 (MSG)

The dream inside of you is more powerful than what you are facing on the outside. After all you have been through, you are still alive. God has preserved you for a higher course. You might know a couple of people who went through half of what you went through or are going through and they didn't survive. But because you are predestined for success, the dream in you kept kicking even when everything around you was shaking.

You may not even know how you made it this far. You may not know what is keeping you strong even when everything around you seems to be going wrong. Friends, you are alive because you have not yet arrived. Just take a look at what you have overcome even in your weakest times. You will realize that you are actually stronger than you think you are. You are a survivor and God preserved you for a divine reason.

Nothing splendid has ever been achieved except by those who dared believe something inside them was superior to their circumstances. [2]
Bruce Barton

Just like a baby is birthed through the process of labor, the pangs and pain you feel today are only signposts heralding your dream dawn. Your best days are ahead of you and not behind you. The dream God put on your inside is superior to your circumstances. What is within you is greater than what is happening outside, even when you feel like you have messed up and missed it.

The Bible says that God has great plans for us (Jer. 29:11). Just in case you have blow plan A, don't worry. God has a plan B, a plan C, a plan D, on and on it goes. Besides, God knows how to make plan B better than the plan A you messed up.

Friends, God is at His best when we are at our worst. He is our peak when we are weak. He is not just the God of Abraham and Isacc. He is the God of Jacob too. Jacob means supplanter, loser, deceiver, liar, and fraudster. Yet God still chose to identify with Jacob, because he had not yet arrived. He had a destiny to fulfill in God's agenda. Hence, Jacob held unto God and wrestled through the night (Gen. 32:24).

No matter where you are or what you've done, God is still willingly to identify Himself with you, if you are willingly to hold unto to Him. Never forget that it is God's grace that protects us to accomplish God's dream in and for our lives. If Grace kept you thus far, it's only because God's dream for your life has not yet been accomplished.

HE'LL STILL USE IT FOR YOUR GOOD

> 'Joseph said, "Let me tell you about my dream. We were out in the field, tying up bundles of wheat. Suddenly my bundle stood up, and your bundles gathered around and bowed down to it. His brothers asked, "Do you really think you are going to be king and rule over us? <u>Now they hated Joseph more than ever because of what he had said about his dream.</u> Joseph later had another dream... Joseph's brothers were jealous of him...'

Genesis 37:6-9,11

Looking at the life of Joseph, we may infer that his brother's hatred triggered the sequence of cataclysmic events in his life. But his brother's hatred was very important in God's strategic plan. It's amazing what God uses to usher us into greatness.

God may not be responsible for every negative event that happens in our life, but He knows how to use every event for our good. He can use our past mistakes, our excuses, our weakness and even our enemies, like we see in Joseph's life.

In the same way Joseph's brothers hated him, when you pinpoint what people hate about you, it may be an indication of where your purpose and worth really is. Antagonistic and critical people often smell greatness in others ahead, even before the carrier knows about it. It was Joseph's brothers that began to make interpretations and deductions about Joseph's dream.

They sensed he was going to be great. They perceived he was a suspect for success, so they hated him. They didn't celebrate his dream with excitement. Perhaps their hatred was only a confirmation that they actually believed his dream would come to pass. Despite their hatred, the Bible records that he still dreamed another dream. Their hatred could not stop the dreams from coming. Eventually, they sold him to the Ishmaelites without knowing that they were paying his fare to the land of his destiny (Gen. 37:28).

Friends, God is still in control no matter what happens. This is a very simple but powerful statement. People that do not realize this try to wrestle and wrangle their way through trails. It's futile to fight God's plan. Flow with it because it always leads to a higher level. You may dislike where you are presently. You may be passing through tough times and it might seem like you have been forgotten sometimes. Your family might even ostracize you. Friends may hate you. Folks may reject you. But remember that God has everything planned out before you were born and your steps are still ordered.

God has made you a wonder. Don't die a wonderer by dancing to the music of people's expectations, personal situations or public opinion. Every sunrise should be a reminder that you have not yet arrived. You didn't wake up because of the alarm clock beside your bed. It was just God's grace. Your eyes can still see, your nostrils can still trap breathe, and your heart can still beat. These are simply divine clues.

Every day is God's way of saying you're alive and still relevant in my global agenda. According to Psalm 150: 6, everything that has breath should praise God, because no matter where you are, God is bound to get the glory. So, there's no need to give up. You might be setback for a season, but when the set time comes, you will know it was all for a reason.

PONDER POINTS

1. God does not give us dreams because they are sensible but because they are possible.

2. Even when we pass through trials and tough times, we should realize that our steps are *still* ordered of God.

3. Most times what we call affliction is simply God's preparation for our promotion.

4. Challenges are not always a sign of negative decisions made in the past. They may be positive indicators of greatness in the future.

5. God is a master strategist. He knows how to use the things that were meant to upset us, to set us up.

6. God's grace is what protects us to accomplish God's dream in and for our lives.

You're Alive Because You've Not Yet Arrived

2

ANY VISION WITHOUT AN OPPOSITION IS AN ILLUSION IN DISGUISE

We live in a society that is designed to keep us within the limits of conformity. There seems to be an invisible box that people's expectation and public opinion have placed us in. For some people, the status quo has become the standard and they would rather sacrifice their dreams to follow the crowd of tradition, popularity and convenience.

But for a real dreamer passionate about making a positive difference, the norm is not normal. They cannot be suppressed or repressed. They often step out and break out because the passion for their dream is stronger than the intimidation of judgmental people.

The pre-birth symptoms of Godly dreams usually manifests in unwillingness to settle for the mundane and mediocre. The dreamer is pregnant with the possibilities of the future and is always eager to stretch beyond walls of conventional thinking into untethered territories and uncharted courses.

Nevertheless, the conceptions of these dream seeds take place during unlikely seasons in our lives. As a result, people wrongly evaluate the authenticity of dreams and visions based on the facts of present reality. If we do not understand this, we will continuously allow ourselves to become prey to the sting of criticism from skeptics and the bite of disapproval from cynics. People have a tendency to always undermine what they do not understand and hurt what they cannot handle.

Once we have God's consent, we should learn to function notwithstanding the disapproval of people. We ought to learn how to be comfortable, even when people do not believe our dream.

> *'For what if some did not believe? shall their unbelief make the faith of God without effect? God forbid: yea, let God be true, but every man a liar...'*
>
> **Romans 3:3-4**

YOU NEED SOME FRICTION TO CLIMB

If you do not have critics, you do not have enough friction to climb the mountain of success. Friction is a very important force in life. Without it, surfaces will be slippery and our stability will be greatly affected. We wouldn't be able to stand, climb, walk, or drive effectively. Even though friction is helpful, it always moves in the opposite direction and is a resisting force.[1]

Comparably, we will always encounter resistance in the course of our destiny. There will be people and situations whose sole purpose is to annihilate, manipulate and assassinate our dream. Just like frictional force is necessary, we need these people in life. For example, Joseph's brothers opposed his dream but they invariably helped to transport him to Egypt. God always uses these people to transport us to our place of destiny.

Being a Godly dreamer has both negative and positive consequences. There will be pillars and caterpillars. There will be mentors and tormentors. There will be advisors and adversaries. So get ready! You cannot be a people pleaser and a goal getter at the same time. Some people will believe in you but some simply will not.

Don't waste your energy on trying to convince *frictional* people to believe you. They always move in the opposing direction. Sometimes, they are more effective for you when they oppose you because they invariably help to stabilize you. Your job is to work out the dream God has given you. The rest is up to God. He knows how to prepare a table in the presence of your enemies.

People need to see you succeed first before calling you a success. This is because they assess you based on your situation. Nevertheless, God calls you a success even before you look like one because he assesses you based on His revelation of you. He knows the future so we can rely on His grace even when the dream doesn't seem possible. Isaiah 46:10 says, *'He declares the end from the beginning.'*

NO RIVAL, NO REVIVAL

There is a problem with your dream if people do not have a problem with it. The flame of revival is often sparked from the friction of rivalry. If everyone supports your vision from day one, it might not really be a vision; it might just be an ambition or illusion. A Godly vision does not always have to be in line with the expectation of people or synchronize with the expertise of the dreamer.

People may not see the chances of its survival or success because of geographic disadvantages and historic antecedents. However, God always selects the least to do the most. He does not want to share His glory with anyone. In reality, we are just channels and He is living His dream through us.

We must learn to swim against the currents of people's expectations if it's not in accordance with God's directions. We see this replicated in the life of Joseph in the book of Genesis 37. As a shepherd boy at 17 years, he had a divine dream and all hell broke loose in the family, to which he seemed oblivious to. But he held on to his dream till it culminated.

Never allow yourself to be intimidated for dreaming. Never permit the fear of men to keep you beneath your potential. Dreamers may not always be popular, but they invariably rule the world. [2]

Pst. Paul Adefarasin

THE DREAM AT 17

I have often wondered why God gave Joseph a dream at the age of 17. Why not at 10, 20 or 35 years? Why did he have the dream at the age of 17? Most theologians try to proffer varied meanings for the biblical significance of the number 17.

Many say it stands for victory over sin because the ark came to rest on the 17th day of the 7 month after the earth was destroyed. Some argue that Christ chronologically rose on the 17th day of the first month. Few state that the number 17 stands for transition because Jacob lived in Egypt for 17 years.[3] In any case, while we may differ in the historical or theological significance of the number 17, we all agree that God is very sequential, systematic and seasonal. He is a God of purpose.

A Suspect For Success: Setback For A Season, Setup For A Reason

Personally, I consider the age 17 as the prime of Joseph's life. Even though he had not yet seen the manifestation of the dream, it was significant because that was the age God planted a seed that would save a generation from extinction.

I do not particularly love Mathematics but I'm going to use it to explain my point. The word *'prime'* is full of meaning, particularly when studied from a mathematical perspective. The number 17 is a prime number and from basic arithmetic, we know that prime numbers can only be divided by themselves and 1.[4] With that understanding we can infer that the number 17 can be divided by only 17 and 1.

While the number 1 represents the unity or sovereignty of God's divinity, the number 17 can be said to represent Joseph (in this context), since this was his present age. Therefore, we can deduce that the dream God gave Joseph at 17, could only be divided, broken down and understood by only Joseph and God. Any other person trying to understand this dream would have reminders of doubt and uncertainty. Just like any other number divided by the number 17 would have remainders.

Hence, the word *prime* in this context is not necessarily a chronological age or biological stage. It's a revelatory phase where everyone may not fully understand your dream, except you and God.

God will always give you a dream in the prime of your life. A time when even though your inner vision contradicts your current situation, you still have the power and passion to pursue what you envision. A time where your present reality is a paradox of your prophecy, yet the fire of your desire is still red hot. That is when you have come to your prime; your 17th year. When God gives you a dream that nobody else would be able to divide, define or decipher. The dream is between you and God.

Perhaps you are wondering why people are not energized about your dream and why they are not responding positively to it. Maybe you are faced with oppositions and afflictions just because of your vision. It is all because you are in your prime. It is your 17th year. So please do not expect your dream to endear you to everybody. You don't need to share your dream with everyone, especially when it is in its budding stage.

The umbilical cord of preference and popularity has to be cut if your dream-baby must live. You cannot be concerned about fitting into people's opinions and still see your dream come true. Often times it's the deepest dream in our heart that causes the greatest tension amongst the ones we love the most, just like we see in Joseph's life. His dream stirred up hatred and animosity within his family.

> 'Now Joseph had a dream, and when he told it to his brothers <u>they hated him even more.</u>'

Genesis 37:5

In this story of Joseph, we see him sharing his dream at the age of 17 with his brothers. But because they couldn't divide, define or decipher his dream completely, there were remains and reminders of hatred, bitterness and envy. Comparably, you may be ostracized, rejected or isolated by family or friends, but if your dream is born of God it will stand the test of time and overcome the world. You don't need people's opinions to see the fruition of your dreams. You need God's approval!

> *You must be too distracted by your future to the point that you don't have any time for your critics.* [5]
> **Apostle Ron Carpenter Jr.**

Criticism is the only way your enemies can explain your success. Only people at your back can back bite you. It's only people that are below your level that have the luxury of time to gossip and criticize you. Sometimes, the best way to know you are a suspect for success and bound to make progress is when people begin to talk about you even before you get to the top, like Joseph's brothers did against him.

As much as we need friction because it helps to stabilize our movements, we must not forget that it is always moving in the opposing direction. We should never drift into its direction; else what was meant to help us ends up hurting us. Don't allow the force of people's opposition to change your direction or water down your passion. Take a look at what Apostle Paul said;

> '... there is a wonderful opportunity for me to do some work here. But there are also many people who are against me.'
> **1 Cor.16:9 (CEV)**

Oppositions are opportunities in disguise. Friends, even Jesus was opposed and rejected when he came for our own good. Get ready; if your vision is from God, it will be tested. Any vision without an opposition is an illusion in disguise.

PONDER POINTS

1. For a real dreamer the norm is not normal; they always stretch beyond walls of conventional thinking.

2. Criticism is the only way your enemies can explain your success.

3. We must learn to swim against the currents of people's expectations if it's not in accordance with God's directions.

4. People need to see you succeed first before they call you a success. This is because they assess you based on your situation. However, God calls you a success even before you look like one because he assesses you based on His revelation of you.

5. If your dream is born of God it will stand the test of time and overcome the world.

6. If you do not have critics, you do not have enough friction to climb the mountain of success.

3

NEVER APOLOGIZE FOR WHAT GOD WANTS YOU TO CELEBRATE OVER

Often times, the need for acceptance drives us to settle for what everyone around is comfortable with. The sense of belonging and the feeling of intimacy we derive from hanging out with little groups and with myopic cliques have a subtle way of blinding us to the enormous weight of destiny we have been entrusted with. This intrinsic thirst of the human soul for overflowing cups of sociological approval and public credence, at the expense of our dreams and destiny has led to more frustrated and unfulfilled people today.

On the other hand, a real dreamer with prospects and potentials; a real dreamer that is a suspect for success understands the language of purpose and revolution. They have the audacity to step out of the comfort of commonality and the security of similarity to answer the clarion call of their calling. A suspect for success would rather become than belong. They would rather become what they were meant to be, than belong where their dreams are suppressed because they do not fit anywhere within the scope of traditional minds.

One of the reasons Joseph was outstanding in life was simply because he knew how to stand out. Besides being the watchdog of the family and giving reports of his brothers to his father, he had a coat of many colors, which his father gave him (Genesis 37: 2-3). This is very important considering the fact that Joseph was very generous and God used him to feed his hungry brothers and starving nations eventually during famine.

However, we see no account of Joseph feeling sorry for his gift or being intimidated to wear his coat before his brothers just because they did not have one. Instead he celebrated it. He wore it before them; he wore it everywhere he went.

> 'Now Israel loved Joseph more than all his children, because he was the son of his old age: <u>and he made him a coat of many colours</u>. And his brethren saw that their father loved him more than all his brethren; and they hated him, and could not speak peaceably unto him.'
> **Genesis 37: 3-4**

Today, many people do not have the audacity and capacity to be singled out for God's blessing. They cannot handle being blessed alone. They feel awkward if they are blessed and everyone else isn't. They feel uneasy sharing their testimony and declaring God's goodness in their lives. They might even be driven to think they are humble and selfless. The truth however is that they are masqueraded with feelings of inadequacy, inferiority and insecurity. These people do not understand the dynamics of God's grace or the ramification of God's blessing.

By celebrating your blessing, you act as an encouragement for others believing God for their own blessings. We need to celebrate what God has given us, like Joseph celebrated the coat his father gave him. It is inferiority not humility that makes us feel uncomfortable about God's gifts and blessings. There is no need to apologize for God's goodness in your life. It's a free gift and it's by His grace.

If you look closely, you will discover that there are people who are very discreet and find it difficult to celebrate what God has given them. These people always get envious and jealous when other people get what they secretly desire or what they think they deserve. The amazing thing is that when they are blessed they remain silent about it, and when others are blessed they are envious about it and want them to be silent about it too.

Friends, we must watch out for those who like Joseph's brothers, specialize in suppressing the talents of prospects and killing the dreams of great people. They are uncomfortable celebrating the success of others and are always pleased with people's dysfunction because that is the level they are on too. They derive their self worth by giving you just enough help and advice to keep you in a needy state, where you would always come back to them. We must not allow these camouflaged opportunists stifle our destiny or suffocate our passion.

EVERYONE HAS A COAT OF MANY COLORS

We all are like Joseph in different aspects. We have a loving Father in heaven that has equipped, endowed and empowered us with *coats* to see our dreams dawn. He has given us different gifts, talents, abilities and graces. There is something within each and every one of us that cannot be duplicated. It was put within us to impact our world and bring glory to God. It's our coat of many colors.

> *'Wherefore he saith, When he ascended up on high, he led captivity captive, and gave gifts unto men.'*
> **Ephesians 4: 8**

One of the greatest expressions of God's extravagant grace is that we all have multiple talents and unique gifts. No one has just one talent. God gave gifts to men. Joseph was an astute shepherd, good housekeeper, anointed dream interpreter and an excellent strategic leader. Friends, believe me when I say your coat has many colors. Your talent has many shades. Your gifting has many expressions. Don't tie yourself to just one area. Discover yourself. Reinvent yourself.

I've seen many businesses that have gone bankrupt because they did not diversify. I've seen award-winning singers fade into oblivion because they did not reinvent themselves. I've seen pastors that are not as impactful as they should be because they have not explored the different colors of their coat.

For instance, if you can preach a message that would change lives, perhaps you can repackage these principles for business solutions in the corporate world. You can also write a book that can change the academic curricula in your community. You can find strategic ways to get your message out. You are multi-colored; you are multi-gifted; you are multi-talented. Use what you have been given!

There are those that would argue that diversifying and exploring the different shades of your gifting would make you unfocused, but I beg to disagree. You can be focused and still be flexible at the same time. Apostle Paul, one of the most impactful preachers said I have become all things to all men, so that they will receive the gospel, (1 Cor. 9:19-23). He was focused and yet flexible.

Usually, it is the different expressions of our grace that ultimately takes us to the height of destiny we envision. Look at David in the

Bible, anointed as king, talented as a musician but still empowered as a warrior. On his way to the throne, he used his skill as a warrior for Goliath, and his talent as a musician for King Saul's mood swings.

What about Joseph? He needed his shepherding skills while he was at home with the sheep. He employed his management acumen in Potiphar's house. He used the dream interpretation grace in his life for Pharaoh's dream and still needed his strategic management expertise while he was on the throne.

One of the reasons I admire Bishop T.D. Jakes is how he has re-invented a *'Woman Thou Art Loosed'* Sunday school curriculum into a powerful sermon, a best-selling book, a widely-acclaimed stage play, a GRAMMY®-nominated music CD, a 2005 NAACP™ Image award movie and an international conference that has drawn more than half a million women from around the world.[1]

These are simply many colors of the same coat. It's the same message, with the same purpose but with a different color and approach. Some people may not appreciate the color of his sermons on the pulpit, but they are captivated by color of his movies or music. It's time to be creative and put on your coat of many colors.

As simple as it sounds, we all must try to be the best person we can: by making the best choices, by making the most of the talents we've been given.[2]
Mary Lou Retton

I must not fail to say that it is one thing to have a coat of many colors; it's another thing to wear it. This is the time to discover, develop and deploy your skill sets. This is time to use what you have. You do not have to be uncomfortable or feel intimidated by the critical chatters of other people who try to silence the exceptionality of your potential. Celebrate who you are and what you have. Put on your coat of many colors. Never apologize to people about the gifts the Father gave you. You have a coat of many colors, put it on!

PONDER POINTS

1. Do not allow the need for acceptance drive you to settle for what everyone around is comfortable with.

2. One of the greatest expressions of God's extravagant grace is that we all have multiple talents and unique gifts.

3. Your talent has many shades. Your gifting has many expressions. Don't tie yourself to just one area. Discover yourself. Reinvent yourself.

4. It is inferiority not humility that makes us feel uncomfortable and ashamed about God's blessings in our life.

5. By celebrating your blessing, you act as an encouragement for others believing God for their own breakthroughs.

6. People who cannot celebrate what God has given them always get envious and jealous when others get what they desire or think they deserve.

Never Apologize For What God Wants You To Celebrate Over

4

THE PAST HAS PASSED; YOUR FUTURE IS NOT IN WHAT YOU LOST, IT'S IN WHO YOU ARE

Anything you cannot change about your past is not a limitation but simply information. I always say, it's better to be an architect of the future rather than an archaeologist of the past. The past does not define us; it only prepares us for the future. One of the greatest tragedies in this generation is that many people have buried their dreams and potentials under the weight of past issues and previous incidents.

Any event after your birth is already too late to define your personality. Your identity stems from divinity; it is not tied to just an activity or experience. You embody the divine makeup and image of God that cannot be distorted by negative incidents or traumatic setbacks. Your worth is based on the reflection of God you represent, not the situations you go through.

Anyone that judges you based on past mistakes or previous misfortunes does so only because they are still living in their past. We run into these people every day, and yet we may still be oblivious to the fact that they are our problem. They constantly remind us of where we failed, but never tell us how to succeed. We may even be deceived into thinking that they love us, because they hang around us all the time.

The simple truth is that they are just comfortable with our present, but threatened by the prospects of our future. You may feel like you bound with them, but the truth is that they only bound with who you were, not who you are presently or who you will be. These people are the poisonous parasites that would rather have you commemorate past memories with them, than create and celebrate a better future without them. They define you based on their perception and expectation, instead of the revelation of your manifestation.

We must be very circumspect, lest in trying to maintain long-time friendships, we unknowingly keep paying allegiance to a dead and toxic relationship that is only comfortable with our today, but too intimidated about our tomorrow.

If you judge me by my past, you're behind schedule. [1]

THAT WAS THEN, BUT THIS IS NOW

Let your past be your motivation, not your limitation. It is not what happened to you, but what is happening in you now that determines what will happen eventually in future. No matter what you have been through in the past, no matter what you lost and what it cost, the fact that you are still alive means that you are more powerful than what you went through. God's grace was sufficient for you.

Your destiny is not tied to your history. It's tied to your decision to learn from the past and make your life count today. God knows how to mix the different unpleasant episodes of your life into the oven of his purpose and cause everything to work together for your good eventually. That is why I always like to say the future is bigger, better and brighter.

A Suspect For Success: Setback For A Season, Setup For A Reason

One of the first of many perils Joseph went through was losing his special coat of many colors. He came to check on his brothers innocently and was stripped of his coat; the symbol of God's favor in his life, the seal of his father's love and the sign of his uniqueness.

> 'And it came to pass when Joseph had come to his brethren, that <u>they stripped Joseph of his coat, his coat of many colors that was on him</u>.'

Genesis 37:23 (Webster)

Let me pause here and ask you, what do you do when you lose what you love? What do you say when you are stripped of what once covered you? Where do you go to when you are separated from what you treasure or cherish? This was where Joseph was and this is exactly where many people are today. You may not see it physically, but a lot of people today are without their coats of many colors.

Everyone has lost someone or something before. It may be a loved one through death, a treasured home through foreclosure, a job through downsizing, a relationship through abuse, a huge investment through a failed business deal or economic recession, or even a special opportunity you always prayed about. Whatever it is, and wherever it happened, the truth is simple; we cannot change the past. We only have today to create the future we dream of.

> *I like the dreams of the future better than the history of the past.* [2]

I am particularly thrilled by Joseph's actions after he lost his coat of many colors. He never struggled to get it back or held a grudge against his brothers. In fact we never hear him mention anything about it throughout his life. He simply let it go and moved on. He forgave them because he realized his future was not in what he lost but who he was.

I need to point out that it was not because Joseph celebrated his coat of many colors that his brother's wanted to kill him. It was his dream they were really after. However, Joseph forgot about the coat and just moved on. He knew that his future was too important to be shackled by bitterness and resentment over the loss of his cherished coat. Joseph had to forgive his brothers to enter into the fullness of his destiny.

Forgiveness is giving yourself permission to succeed. I love the way Nurisha Liggins puts it. She says, *'forgiveness means I love myself enough to release you from damaging me further'.*[3] Forgiveness unlocks the future we envision. There are things we should just let go, if we must move forward in life. It is not always easy, but it's necessary, if we must see our dreams dawn. So dry your tears, learn your lessons and maximize your life today.

Apostle Paul admonishes us to reach forward to our future by forgetting the past. Unforgiveness is a bondage we have to break free from. We have to learn to not only forgive others when they hurt us but to forgive ourselves when we hurt other people. Else we live a life full of regret and guilt. This was one of the keys that made Apostle Paul forgive himself after a brutal past of murder, massacre and manslaughter to become one of the greatest apostles.

> 'This one thing I do, <u>forgetting those things which are behind</u>, and reaching forth unto those things which are before.'
> **Philippians 3:13**

THE PAST ... YOUR MESSAGE OR YOUR BONDAGE

Your past either becomes your message or your bondage overtime. A good illustration is fire. Fire is very productive and can be used for cooking, warming our homes, etc. But when it is out of control, it becomes destructive and can result to wildfires amongst other damages.

Like fire, the past can be a good servant if you master how to use it productively and effectively to help others. But it can also become destructive if is out of control and detects our thought and actions. Pain from previous experiences should incubate the passion and willingness to change. It is not supposed to be the tomb of our dreams or the sepulcher of our aspirations.

The past is not for continual residence but for positive reference. Joel Osteen once said, 'Whatever happened in the past, happened for you not to you'.[5] We should be proactive, not reactive to the past. We should learn from experiences, but we must not live in them. If we keep regretting, we keep regressing. There is no need to reside in a past we can't reverse. If you keep giving it attention, it will give you direction.

My past is not my project. It was my school.[6]
Dr. Mike Murdock

Like Joseph, we must learn to let go and move on. Your future is not in what you lost, it is who you are. Do not become hostage to the painful circumstances of the past and limit the possibilities of your future. Quit visiting the mortuary of the past to embalm the dead issues of your life. New things do not happen till there is a vacancy created in your life. You must give your future an opportunity to manifest by forgiving yourself and any other person that you hinge the blame of the past on.

Perhaps, you were or are into secret habits, it is time to ask God for forgiveness. Accept God's grace and stop feeling guilty about it. It is time to move on. You might have gone through a failed marriage, a broken relationship or a career setback. Whatever it is, I want you to know that God is set to do new things in your life if you will only look up and move out. Let the past be in the past, God wants to do a new thing in your life today.

> '... *Don't cling to events of the past* or dwell on what happened long ago. *Watch for the new thing I am going to do*. It is happening already- you can see it now...'
> **Isaiah 43:18-19 (GNT)**

This is your season and you have to take advantage of the time you have today. Time is one of the greatest gifts of life given to change history and create possibilities. In it, the past is buried, the present is sown and the future is nurtured. You must make a demarcation from your past to have a connection to your future. People have gone through worse situations and still overcome them to become successful.

Do not let your past be an excuse, make it your reason to succeed. Whatever is lost and dead in your life will be the soil in which your future will germinate. You are pregnant with destiny. That is why God sustained you through the night. It is time to step into your purpose and defy the fear of the unknown, unseen and undone.

A Suspect For Success: Setback For A Season, Setup For A Reason

The past has passed, you may have lost your coat of many colors like Joseph, but no matter where and what you go through, the dream is still within you. The future is not in what you lost. It's not in the past. It's in who you are today.

PONDER POINTS

1. Anything you cannot change about your past is not a limitation but simply information.

2. Any event after your birth is already too late to define your personality. Your worth is based on the reflection of God you represent, not the situations you go through.

3. The past doesn't confine you from the future. It only refines you for the future.

4. Forgiveness is giving yourself permission to succeed. We have to learn to not only forgive others when they hurt us but to forgive ourselves when we hurt other people.

5. It's better to be an architect of the future rather than an archaeologist of the past.

6. Your past either becomes your message or your bondage. Either your motivation or your limitation. Either your excuse to fail or your reason to succeed. Many people have gone through worse situations and still made it.

5

TREASURE YOUR TRIALS; HURTFUL SITUATIONS OFTEN BIRTH HELPFUL CONNECTIONS

The pain of unexpected seasons and unwanted trials can be so overwhelming that it blindfolds us to their intended purpose. There are times when it seems like the pressures of life blankets the horizons of our expectations and shrouds the landscape of our aspirations. Leaving us to maneuver and meander through dark potholes and pitfalls. These are the times where it feels like God has just forgotten us. These can be trying times and crying times, but these are also turning points and defining moments.

Our experiences don't surprise God; neither do our setbacks shock Him. God is in control of whatever we are going through. If God is not working on something for you, then He is always working on you for something. This is where faith comes in. You may not feel or see what God is doing, but that does not negate the fact that he is working behind the scenes for your good.

I do not know of anyone who suffered more calamity than Job in the Bible. Yet after losing all he had, when it all did not make sense and he could not see God's hand in what he was going through, he still said;

> '*I cannot find God anywhere-- in front or back of me, to my left or my right. God is always at work, though I never see him.*'
> **Job 23:8-9 (CEV)**

Friends, this should be our attitude. No matter where you are or what you are going through now, you can say like Job, I may not be able to see what God is doing through all this but I believe He is always at work in my life. This is the faith that cripples the enemies' schemes and strategies. This is the faith that changes our fate.

Faith in God empowers us to takes our eyes off what we are going through and align ourselves to seek God's purpose for the season we are in. Faith always positions us for divine opportunity in adverse situations.

When you find yourself going through seasons of trials and it seems like God is silent, always remember this analogy. Silence during a test doesn't denote the absence of teachers or supervisors. On the contrary, it indicates their confidence and presence. It proves that they believe in the capacity of the students and have given them an opportunity to pass the test that would qualify them for promotion.

Just like the pit, the prison was also a test for Joseph. After Joseph was falsely accused and thrown into the prison, he must have felt abandoned, forgotten and forsaken. He must have concluded that God was silent. But God was not silent. He was still at work even though Joseph didn't see him. He was with Joseph in the prison working behind the scenes.

Perhaps Joseph must have breathed a sigh of relief after going through the pit to becoming Potiphar's servant. He must have thought his dream was about to unfold. Potiphar's house did not resemble the palace but at least it was close to corridors of power; Potiphar was the captain of Pharaoh's guards. But God had another plan. He wanted

Joseph to go through the prison because he had to make some useful relationships that would propel him to the palace.

Many people have missed out on relationships that would have catapulted them into momentous realms because they lived by assumptions; having their eyes blinded and paths darkened by lack of illumination that comes with discovery of purpose. [1]

CONNECTED THROUGH CRISES

We must learn to treasure our trials and value our pain, because God often uses these unpleasant and hurtful situations to birth helpful connections. You may need to change your perspective. Your miracle might be around you. Today, many people are seeking for connections and opportunities to actualize their dreams.

However, like Joseph, the connections and networks you need to unlock your destiny may not be in the palace (where you do not have access to) but in the prison (where you may be now). We live in a world where people seem unreachable because of the barriers of hierarchy, security or status, yet God knows how to connect people with and through crises.

In Genesis 40, Joseph met Pharaoh's chief butler in prison and after he interpreted his dream, he was released. Years later, he (the chief butler) mentioned Joseph to Pharaoh who needed an interpreter for his (Pharaoh) own dream.

> *'Then spake the chief butler unto Pharaoh, saying… <u>there was there with us a young man, an Hebrew, servant to the captain of the guard… he interpreted to us our dreams</u>… And it came to pass, as he interpreted to us… Then Pharaoh sent and called Joseph, and they brought him hastily out of the dungeon…'*

Genesis 41: 9-14

Cherish your challenges and treasure your trials. I met my beautiful wife while I was going through a very painful and difficult period in my life. With all I was going through I was not praying for a wife at that moment. I just wanted God to see me through the traumatic season I was facing. I believe that God wanted me to go through it, because he wanted me to meet my wife. Friends, God knows how to birth helpful connections from painful situations.

Joseph met the chief butler in the prison. Ruth met Boaz in the midst of famine and pain (Ruth 1, 2). David met King Saul for the first time in a battle with Goliath (I Sam. 17). As a matter of fact, most miracles in the Bible happened to people who met the Lord when they were at their wits end. Their situation gave birth to the divine connection they needed for their solution. Peter met Jesus after he had toiled all night and caught nothing (Luke 5:5). The blind man at the Temple gate met Peter and John while they were going to pray (Acts 3:1-7).

Do you really know why you are where you are? Most times God allows us to go through adverse predicaments not only to shape our character but to connect us to the right people we will need in future. Had Joseph been consumed with his situation in prison, he wouldn't have offered to help the chief butler interpret his dream (Genesis 40:6-23). Quit bemoaning your situation and open your eyes. You never know who is next to you; that might just be your spring board to your dream dawn.

Adversity draws men together and produces beauty and harmony in life's relationships... [2]

Soren Kierkegaard

God uses relationships to usher us into a new season and that is why the enemy's greatest attack is against relationships; our relationship with God, our spouse, our family members, loved ones and people we meet every day. The devil never attacked Adam till there was an Eve in his life. The devil attacked that relationship because they had the key of dominion, and he is still doing that today. God said in Genesis 1:26, Let *them* have dominion. He was not just referring to mankind, but the relationship between Adam and Eve.

Every successful person today is a product of divine connection and relationship. Every Ruth needs a Naomi. Every Elisha needs an Elijah. Every Joshua needs a Moses. Every Mary needs an Elizabeth. Even Jesus needed John the Baptist to announce His arrival and His disciples to work with Him.

No matter how much you pray, fast or sow seeds you still need people; you cannot make it alone. Although David was anointed for the throne, I believe he needed Jonathan to learn palace ethics and kingly mannerisms. Success in life is all about relationships. It's about working with and meeting the right people, and you don't know where you will meet them.

Treasure Your Trials, Hurtful Situations Births Helpful Connections

Personal relationships are the fertile soil from which all advancement, all success, all achievement in real life grows. [3]

Ben Stein

Today, I want to encourage you to be optimistic; change your perspective towards adversity. Most people want a relationship with the *Pharaohs* of Success above, yet have not treated the people around them well, because they don't look like a success. But often times these people around us are the *Chief Butlers* that will connect us to the top.

Do not be so sympathetic, drunk and obsessed with your issues that you forget you can be a fountain of hope and solution for others. The pain, predicament and problem you are going through might create the right partnership you require for the palace. You can never get to the top alone. Trust God, seize opportunities around you and link your way out of where you are to where you want to be. It's your network that will make the dream work.

PONDER POINTS

1. God allows us to go through adverse predicaments not only to shape our character but to connect us to the right people we will need in future.

2. Faith in God empowers us to takes our eyes off what we are going through and align ourselves to seek God's purpose for the season we are in.

3. Silence during life's test doesn't denote God's absence but his presence. It proves that God believes in your capacity and has given you an opportunity to pass the test that would qualify you for promotion.

4. God knows how to connect people with and through crises.

5. Do not be so sympathetic, drunk and obsessed with your issues that you forget you can be a fountain of hope and solution for others.

6. The enemy's greatest attack is against our relationships with God, our spouse, our family members, loved ones and people we meet every day. This is because God uses relationships to usher us into a new season.

6

YOUR REAL MEASURE IS REVEALED UNDER PRESSURE

We live in a generation plagued with a dearth of integrity and responsibility. Today, it seems like we all are standing at the shores of indifference and impropriety. We stare as our core values and essential principles are eroded by the rapid surge of compromise, corruption and carnality sweeping through the foundations of our tenets. Having a good reputation is swiftly going into extinction and success is no longer synonymous with character. Words like ethics and accountability and are no longer appealing to a society whose moral compass seem to be skewed.

We need to realize that a dream only shows you what the future holds, but character is what holds you till and when you get to the future you envision. Character is everything. What you see about your future is always at the mercy of who you really are. A vision is only the picture of the future but character is the structure of that picture. It's the frame that sustains that picture in your spirit; it keeps you where the dream will take you to.

There are many people who have aborted their destinies. They had great talents and gifts; they saw a bright future ahead, but they never took the time to develop the character that would sustain what they had seen. This is seen in the popular story of Samson that compromised his character in the face of pressure from Delilah (Judges 16).

The collapse of character begins with compromise. [1]

Pst. John Hagee

How many dreamers are still locked up behind bars because they compromised their integrity when it mattered the most? How many people are heartbroken today because they dreamed of a great wedding but failed to develop great character for the marriage? How many people have been helpless victims of abuse and exploitation by those they trusted and believed in? How many people are trapped in the vicious cycle of regret and guilt because they didn't say NO to the momentary advances of sensuality or the fading gloss of temptation?

How many people have constantly blown unimaginable opportunities they had because of an inappropriate action stemming from a weak character framework? All around us we see people dreaming of success but doing nothing about their ethics and ethos. Your purpose is given to you by God, but you develop the character to sustain it before success can be achieved. Make no mistake about this; character is very key in achieving sustainable impact in life. It is not just about right confession; it's about right action under pressure.

You cannot dream yourself into a character; you must hammer and forge yourself one. [2]

James A. Froude

It takes the fruit of the Spirit (Godly character, Gal. 5:22-23) to keep you where the gift of the Spirit has taken you to. Your gift can make a way for you, but your character sustains you at the top. God promotes the faithful not the famous (Matthew 25:21). God rewards character not charisma. The gift of the Spirit in Joseph's life was very evident. He had been given the gift of leadership and management. The Spirit of prosperity in his life was apparent, but he had to develop his character. His character was tested and tried; he had to learn faith in the pit, patience in the prison, and purity through Portiphar's wife, before he could be trusted with the power of the palace.

'And after a time, <u>his master's wife, looking on Joseph with desire, said to him, Be my lover</u>. But he would not, and said to her... <u>how then may I do this great wrong, sinning against God</u>? And day after day she went on requesting Joseph to come to her and be her lover, but he would not give ear to her. Now one day he went into the house to do his work; and not one of the men of the house was inside. And pulling at his coat, she said, Come to my bed; but slipping out of his coat, he went running away.'
Genesis 39:7-12

THE PRESSURE OF PLEASURE

Evang. Dwight L. Moody said, *'character is what a man is in the dark'*. [3] What you are in the dark determines how and if you will shine. Just like orange juice is released by squeezing an orange fruit, the real measure of a man is revealed in the dark, under pressure. That is when, where and how we know the stuff you are made off. When you seem discouraged, depressed and despondent and life coerces you to a tight corner, how do you respond? This is the real test of who you are.

Nevertheless, understand that pressure is not always stressful, difficult or burdensome. Sometimes pressure can be pleasure. It can be an issue of gratification, freedom, desire, position and power. Character is also revealed in a position of affluence and influence. You may never really know people till they are at the top.

Look at Joseph, as a slave, he was still prosperous. He was in charge of everything and everyone. Yet he did not get intoxicated with the wine of lustful persuasion, instead he told Potipahar's wife NO. Most people today would jump on this death trap disguised as momentary opportunity. But Joseph knew that the measure of a man is revealed under pressure. If God can trust you when you are down, then he will thrust you up eventually.

> *Not everything with wings is an eagle. Try them by the height of their character.* [4]

Nurisha Liggins

A good character will always produce the right attitude in situations. The right attitude will get you to the desired altitude eventually. Solomon said that a good name is better than riches (Proverbs 22:1). There are people today who are willing to ruin their reputation to change their situation, and are expecting to make progress in life. While this might bring instant success, it is only passing not permanent.

Friends, it's time to go back to the basics; a Godly character is an essential principle for sustaining success and leaving a lasting legacy. It may not be popular or fashionable but it is important and acceptable to God. Paul understood this principle of character and the power of discipline. Little wonder he became one of the greatest apostles who ever lived. Consider what he said;

> *'You know what you must do to imitate us. We lived a disciplined life among you.'*
> **2 Thes. 3:7(GW)**

Do you have a dream in your spirit that has not yet manifested? This is the right time to develop the character and discipline to sustain your dream. Yes, now is the right time, before the spotlight of fame turns on you and your actions are judged in the court of public opinion. Now is the right time, while you are in the pit and prison like Joseph and nobody knows you. This is the right time to develop yourself and do what you have to do; this process is a preparatory season.

You may need to study or pray more hours, you may need to work on your tongue and manners, you may need to be more patient and loving, you may need to stop procrastinating and be more time conscious or you may need to exercise more or eat healthy. Whatever it is, learn to work on yourself to maturity and responsibility, so that when the pressure of success comes, you will be unshaken. You can only change the world when you have changed yourself.

> *'But I discipline my body and keep it under control, lest after preaching to others I myself should be disqualified.'*
> **I Cor. 9:27 (ESV)**

PONDER POINTS

1. If God can trust you when you are down, then he will thrust you up eventually.

2. A vision is only the picture of the future but character is the structure of that picture.

3. It takes the fruit of the Spirit (character) to keep you where the gift of the Spirit has placed you.

4. God promotes the faithful not the famous. He rewards character not charisma.

5. You can only change the world when you have changed yourself.

6. Character is more than right confession. It involves right action under pressure.

7
ISOLATION IS NOT REJECTION, BUT PREPARATION FOR PROMOTION

We are social beings created for relationships. Right from the very moment we make our grand entrance into the world as infants, we find ourselves depending on people for attention, affirmation and affection.

Overtime, our need for dependency seemingly wanes when we outgrow juvenile stages in life. However, our inherent communal craving for relationships is transferred to the workplace, church and other ventures we find ourselves in. Today, the world has become a global village because of the social media and Internet.

We have discovered the strength of synergy and leveraged on the benefits of partnership. Treaties have been formed between nations. Unions have been formed between people of shared interest. Businesses have formed strategic pacts. Organizations have signed agreements to protect their investments. We are harnessing the enormous power of mutual cooperation that ensures collective success.

However, God does not need to partner with everyone to make a difference. He does not begin a revolution with the mass or multitude. He just needs one man that can make the difference. He needs one man that is willing to walk with Him and work with Him. Walk with Him through the lonely night when the dream seems impractical. Work with Him through the pain and perils when the vision seems impossible. The man that God partners with is the man that is willing to take the risk to believe Him, even if it means standing alone.

Please do not misunderstand me, I'm a strong proponent of having powerful connections and networks. I pointed out in an earlier chapter, that God births helpful connections out of hurtful situations. But there are some battles you have to fight alone. There is a limit to which recommendations from people and partnership can take you to, after which you are on your own. There are some challenges in life you will have to experience personally to become a testimony. Just like Jacob, sometimes you may have to wrestle alone to change your destiny.

> *'And Jacob was left alone; and there wrestled a man with him until the breaking of the day... And he said, Thy name shall be called no more Jacob, but Israel: for as a prince hast thou power with God and with men, and hast prevailed.'*
> **Genesis 32:24, 28**

During my masters program in the United Kingdom, we were encouraged and allowed to study in groups prior to our finals. We asked ourselves potential exam questions and we exchanged useful information that was beneficial to all of us. But when the D-day came, we weren't sitting in groups anymore; we all had to sit alone and answer the questions alone. We had to go through this exam experience to be qualified for the next level academically.

Likewise, there are some tests in life you have to go through alone for promotion, no matter the company of assistance you had during the preparation. Many people have the proclivity to think that everything will be rosy just because they have a dream. I've realized that God often allows us to dream about the prospects and possibilities of our future. This develops the passion that sustains us till we synchronize with the promise. We hardly ever dream about the preparation and process. Joseph never dreamt of the pit and prison; he only dreamt about the palace and his brothers bowing to him.

> 'And they took him (Joseph) and threw him into a pit. <u>The pit was empty;</u> there was no water in it.'
> **Genesis 37:24**

Isolation is often times the incubator for revelation. God uses isolation to provide direction, produce distinction and propel us to our destination. Joseph was thrown into the pit alone. He was not with any friend or relative, he was there alone. He didn't have anyone to talk to, but God. It was an exam he had to take alone to be admitted into the land where his dreams would materialize. It was part of the curriculum of God's agenda to transport him into Egypt. The pit was part of the divine plan, even though it was not part of Joseph's dream at 17.

I have often wondered why Joseph did not struggle with his brothers. Perhaps he was in shock by his brother's horrendous acts or maybe he had given up on his dreams. Perchance it could be that he totally trusted God to deliver him or possibly he was overpowered by his elder brothers? Whatever it was, the simple fact was that Joseph was now in the pit, alone.

How does a passionate dreamer feel in a dry pit? How does a great man feel in a dark place? How did Joseph really feel? Just days ago, he was excited about his unbelievable dream, and now here he was, inside a pit, at the mercy of his brother's envy and hatred.

What do you do when what you saw about your future contradicts what is happening presently? How do you feel when what you expect is not what you experience? Where is the strength to face the day when your current position does not tally with your divine prophecy? Where do you go to when the realities of life tends to dampen the excitement of your dream? What do you do when your heart has been broken by someone you poured your life into, and here you are alone in the pit of loneliness?

P.I.T ... PREPARATION. INSTRUCTION. TRANSITION

Friends, I have good news for you. The pit is a place of preparation, instruction and transition (P.I.T). You will not die in the pit. It is the boardroom where you get the strategy for the palace. Isolation doesn't mean that God has rejected you, even if people have. If anyone walked out on you, then they really didn't belong to your future. It doesn't always mean something is wrong with you; in fact it might just be the opposite.

Take advantage of where you are now. God has brought you to a place where He has your full attention, so He can give you direction. God allows certain situations in our life to develop our capacity to handle what He has put in our spirit. Joseph, the excited dreamer learnt faith and patience in the pit. He learnt to walk by faith and not by sight. When he could not trace God, he learnt to trust him. He learnt the guidance of God's silence.

Many people today are in Joseph's shoes; trapped in a pit with only a glimpse of their dream. There are many blessed people with great dreams, incredible gifts and amazing talents that are stuck in the pit of life, shielded from the sunlight of their dreams.

Understand that it is not uncommon for great men to be in strange and unfamiliar seasons; in fact it is actually necessary. Great people often go through conflicting seasons that have no correlation to where and what they want to be in the future. In this season, they learn divine direction, faith and patience. They are prepared, instructed and ready to transition to the next level. They learn to stop looking at what they are going through and focus on where you are going to. The logic is simple; if you can't trust God in the pit then why should He trust you with or thrust you to the palace?

PREPARED AND PRESERVED IN SECRET

Time would fail me to talk about David. He was the shepherd feeding his father's sheep as a young man in the bush after he was anointed by God to be king over Israel (I Sam. 16: 13, 1 Sam. 17: 15). Most people think that after the anointing comes the throne, or like Joseph, after the dream comes the reality, but this is not always so. There is always a process. This is the season we get our testimony and song.

David wrote many of the psalms we read today when he was alone or running from danger. David killed bears and lions when he was alone, and that gave him the boldness to kill Goliath in public. A lot of people want to get to the top without any evidence or testimony of what they had to overcome secretly.

Just like Joseph learnt faith and patience, David learnt direction in the wilderness. No wonder he said that even in the valley of the shadow of death he feared no evil because God was his shepherd (Psalm 23:1,4). I ask today, what have or are you learning today? Isolation is an essential part of preparation. You can never be praised publicly for what you never practiced and prepared for privately.

Sometimes you have to stay alone, to stay above. A vision is not enough; you need direction from God. You need to be alone with God to get the full blueprint. Often times when we are too busy, God will use the situations we dislike to bring us to our knees to seek him for directions. Other times, it would be to develop the character to support the dream we have.

Sometimes you need to recharge privately before you can discharge publicly. Hibernation for rejuvenation is very necessary for Success in life.

Pst. Abimbola Komolafe

The stigma of Jacob's name on his destiny drove him to wrestle alone with God all-night because he needed to be blessed and empowered (Genesis 32:24). Trouble has a way of driving us close to God, especially when we get too preoccupied with activities. We must not wait for situations to spend time with God; it should be a deep desire that flows out of a genuine relationship. Sometimes you just need to turn off the TV, switch off the phones and iPads™, shut down the computers, cancel the appointments and separate yourself to seek God's face.

You won't reach your altitude always walking with the multitude. The place of isolation is a place of revelation, rejuvenation and restoration. It is a must if you must succeed. I once heard Dr. Mike Murdock say that most of the ideas he got that made him successful were gotten during his quiet time with the Lord. Friends, if you are too busy to be alone with God, then you are too busy to succeed. Hours with God makes minutes with men productive.

> *'And when <u>he had sent the multitudes away</u>, he went up into a mountain apart to pray: and when the evening was come, <u>he was there alone</u>.'*
>
> **Matthew 14:23**

I believe that God used the pit to also preserve Joseph till the Midianite traders going to Egypt passed by and he was sold into their hands (Genesis 37:28). Perhaps Joseph was feeling like he was forgotten by God in that pit, but what he did not know was that he was preserved by God for destiny. Had he gotten into the wrong trader's hand, he would not have been sold into Potiphar's house. This would mean he would not have gone into the prison to interpret the dream of the cup bearer and baker, and ultimately never have gotten to the palace.

Do not be afraid of the pit. It is just a phase. Learn what you need to learn and move on. Like David, kill those lions in the wilderness and write those psalms. Before you know it, you'll be before King Saul. Like Joseph, trust God and do not be discouraged when you cannot figure out how the dream picture will all come together. Your role is simply to believe God and walk by faith. Do not feel left out when the people you started with seem to have left you behind. You are simply prepared and preserved for destiny. You won't die in that pit. You will come out and fulfill your destiny.

PONDER POINTS

1. Isolation is an essential part of preparation. You can never be praised publicly for what you never practiced and prepared for privately.

2. If you want God to thrust you to the palace, you have to learn to trust him in the pit.

3. The P.I.T means Preparation, Instruction and Transition. God uses it to provide direction, produce distinction in our life and propel us to our destination.

4. You won't reach your altitude always walking with the multitudes.

5. God allows certain situations in our life to develop our capacity to handle what He has put in our spirit.

6. Great people often go through conflicting seasons that have no correlation to where and what they want to be in the future. In this season, they learn divine direction, faith and patience.

8

SITUATIONS ARE MEANT TO REFINE YOU, NOT DEFINE YOU

Our society is programmed to celebrate only finished products. Finished products that have pioneered amazing discoveries, displayed outstanding results, accomplished extraordinary feats or amassed great fortune. Many have applauded them as heroes and role models, some have labeled them celebrities and superstars and others have branded them as legends and genius.

While we may differ in what we choose to call them, we certainly concur that they all have somewhat broken through the cocoon of mediocrity in their respective fields and hit amazing high notes in life's musical scale of accomplishment.

However, somewhere in-between the loud ovations and long applause, we often seem oblivious to the fact that it took the furnace of time, trials and transformation to purify these people into what we treasure today. No one was born with accolades, accomplishments or achievements attached to their waists from their mother's womb.

There is always a process to progress in life and God will always use situations to refine us for our ultimate destiny. Most times God will do some things *in* you first, before he can do some things *for* you. Let your situation refine you. Let it prepare you. Don't make it an excuse, instead make it the reason to succeed. One of my favorite verses in the Bible is;

Situations Are Meant To Refine You, Not Define You

> 'But he knoweth the way that I take: when he hath tried me, <u>I shall come forth as gold.</u>'

Job 23:10

Do not define yourself based on what you are going through; instead define yourself based on where you are going to. If you refuse to be refined by situations, you'll be confined by them. Whatever didn't defeat you can only make you stronger. No matter what you're passing through now, it will lead you to a place of purification and perfection if you believe God. The circumstance you're facing is not permanent; the only thing permanent is God's word. Weeping is for the night, but when the morning comes the mourning ceases because joy comes.

THE BLESSING IS IN THE STRESSING

Friends, the miracle you are believing God for may be hidden in the crises you're currently dealing with. Goliath might have been seen as a symbol of Israel's fear or defeat. But in reality he was just a precursor for David's greatness (1 Sam. 17).

> 'We <u>went through fire and flood</u>, but you <u>brought us to a place</u> of great abundance.'

Psalm 66:12(NLT)

Notice in that verse that *fire and flood* is a phase, because it says, *we went through.* But *great abundance* is a place because that is where we are brought to. You have to go through some things to get to the fullness of your purpose. There are some dimensions of multiplication that you may never encounter till you go through afflictions because the fire and the flood give us the capacity to handle great abundance.

'But the more they afflicted them, the more they multiplied and grew...'

Exodus 1:12

The Israelites had to be afflicted before they multiplied exceedingly (Exodus 1:12). Daniel faced the lion's den before he qualified for prosperity in the reign of king Darius (Daniel 6). Even Jesus had to go through Calvary before He completed his assignment. Never confuse your temporary phase, with your permanent place.

I once read in a medical article that the vaccine of a particular disease is made from the toxin that causes it. This means that cure is in the cause. Similarly in life, the solution you seek might be in that situation you are going through. The blessing comes from the stressing. The New Testament church in Acts never grew in grace, revival and impact till God scattered them through contention and persecution, (Acts 19:11). If there is no rival, there is no revival. You have to go through the *stress* of the pit and the prison to get to the blessing of the palace.

The Grace of God upon our life sometimes attracts challenges and even afflictions. [1]

Rev. Henry Emmanuel

THE PIT WAS THE REAL TEST OF LEADERSHIP, NOT THE PALACE.

Has it ever occurred to you that in every season of setback Joseph went through, he was promoted to the place of leadership except the pit? In prison, he was made the leader of the prisoners. In Potiphar's house, he was put in charge of everything and everyone. However, in the pit, he was alone.

I believe the ultimate test of the pit was not really how he handled being betrayed by his brothers, but how he led and managed himself while he was in the pit alone. In God's curriculum, Joseph wouldn't have passed to the level of managing Potiphar's house or the prisoners, if he didn't know how to lead and manage himself when he was alone. If he couldn't manage the pit, he would never have made it to the palace. The pit was the first and real test of leadership.

True leadership is not only about what you do when you are surrounded by people that support you. It is what you do when no one is around, no one believes in you and you have been betrayed. True leadership is holding onto your dream, even when there seems to be no way out. It is when you have the fortitude to encourage yourself like David did (1 Sam. 30:6), and refuse to allow your condition to determine your reaction. This is because you have a vision and it has not yet come to pass. True leadership is about leading yourself when there is no one and nothing to signal the dawn of better things to come.

Joseph was in the dark pit alone, like Jesus was in the tomb for three days. Joseph was restricted in mobility, yet still connected by destiny. He was limited in space, yet he was at the right place. Isn't it amazing how things can be tight and tough, yet God has us just where he needs us- in the pit? Friends, it's only a test. If you are irritated or frustrated in the pit, it could mean that your excitement is only superficial and tied to things and people. When you are separated from people in the pit, your coat of many colors is stripped from you, and you are still passionate and optimistic about your dreams, you are then ready for the next level.

POTIPHAR'S HOUSE -TRANSITION, NOT DESTINATION

Many people only see Joseph's stay in Potiphar's house as a test of his loyalty to God when he refused to sleep with Potiphar's wife. Nonetheless, God also put Joseph in charge of everything in Potiphar's house because he wanted to test his faithfulness when entrusted with little things.

Faithfulness is the bridge of transition that leads us to our destination. If Joseph could not manage Potiphar's house, how could he have managed the nation of Egypt? Many people have great destines but they fail to realize that little keys open great doors. Despise not the days of little beginning (Zach. 4:10). Nothing great starts big. If you are not willing to be faithful in little things, then you are not willing to be fruitful with big things. How you handle the small things ultimately reflects how you will handle the big things. Look at what Jesus said;

> '... thou good and faithful servant: thou hast been _faithful over a few things, I will make thee ruler over many things..._ '
>
> **Mathew 25:21**

THE PRISON WAS ONLY A 'PRE-SEASON' TO THE PALACE.

'He (The Warden) put Joseph in charge of all the other prisoners and made him responsible for everything that was done in the prison'

Genesis 39:22(GNT)

How does a prisoner lead other prisoners? How can you manage inmates when you are one of them? How do you manage people that have the same issues you have and struggle with the same things you struggle with? Here was Joseph, a prisoner, yet still leading other prisoners. How is it that God placed Joseph in a position where he had to nurse people that were bleeding in the same place he was bleeding? This is the test of the prison.

Your ability to be a solution to people regardless of what did or didn't work in your life is important to your destiny. God never calls perfect people, He calls great people. You will always have issues, but we must not be so preoccupied with our issues that we forget that we can offer help to others.

In the prison, the Bible says God was there, with Joseph. God is not just there to help you; He also wants to know how you treat people that are seemingly nobodies. How do you manage people or things that are below your level of expertise? How do you handle being at a stage where you are overqualified for?

Prisoners are people confined and punished for their past crimes. So the question is, how do you handle people with unpleasant past experiences? How do you handle people that have messed up and missed it? How do you handle people with issues and struggles? How do you relate with them?

Are you concerned about their feelings and disposition like Joseph was? Do you help people just because you need a favor in return or just because you want to be a blessing?

Finally, how do you react when the people you help, forget you just like the Chief Butler forgot Joseph. These are questions we should ask ourselves when we feel like we are stuck in the prison of life. When we allow God to process us, then He will, in time, move us out of the pre-season (prison) stage into the fullness of our season.

SEE THE BIG PICTURE

Those who see the ultimate cannot be intimidated by the immediate. If you see the big picture of joy set before you, you would develop the tenacity to hang on till you synchronize with your promise. Jesus endured the cross because of the picture of the Joy set before him (Heb. 12:2). If you can trust God in the test, he will make you come out as the best. Job said that when he had gone through the fire he would come out as gold. You have to go through the fire to be on fire for God. Purified gold comes after the fire and not before the fire.

Look at Joseph, he had to go through the pit and prison, but he didn't allow his situation to define him; instead his dream defined him. He saw the big picture.

> *'He sent a man before them, even Joseph, who was sold for a servant: Whose feet they hurt with fetters: he was laid in iron: <u>Until the time that his word came</u>: the word of the LORD tried him. <u>The king sent and loosed him</u>; even the ruler of the people, and let him go free. He made him lord of his house, and ruler of all his substance.'*

Psalm 105:17-22 (Webster)

Growing up in Nigeria as a child, I always played with my siblings and neighbors most evenings. One of our favorite pastimes aside playing soccer was plucking fruits from the orange trees in front of our house. We spotted ripe fruits and threw large stones at them, hoping that they would fall off, and they usually did. The only reason we threw stones at a particular fruit was because it was ripe. If it wasn't ripe and ready, it was not worth our effort, time or stones.

Recently, as I told my wife this story it dawned on me that sometimes life can be likened to children plucking ripe fruits. The most fruitful are the most attacked. Just like we threw stones only at the ripe fruits, most people loaded with potentials, prospects and possibilities are under severe attack from every corner. They are ripe for harvest but find themselves in serious crises.

If we see the big picture, we will realize that the severity of tests and trials we face serve as an indication that we are ripe and ready for greatness. The attack does not mean you are not in the will of God. It means you are ready to come into the fullness of your destiny. We should not allow setbacks to poison our dream seeds with skepticisim and unbelief. Rather we must rise up in faith because the manifestation of our dream is closer than it has ever been before.

When you call a situation hopeless, you empower the enemy to hinder your deliverance. Hope is not denial of affliction; it is the anticipation of freedom.²

This is harvest time; it's not the time to quit. Don't condemn yourself or feel like you are cursed because of what you are going through. There is nothing wrong with you, instead there is something right with you. You are a suspect for success. The time is right and you are ripe, it's about time for your change.

THE OPPORTUNITY OF ADVERSITY

Most people abort their dreams with their confessions during their season of preparation and testing. If you consider Joseph's life, you would discover that he didn't speak much, even when he was thrown into the pit and prison. There was no record of him saying anything negative. He only spoke about four things before he came face to face with Pharaoh.

He spoke about dreams, direction, devotion and disposition. He shared his *dream* with his brothers. He asked for *direction* when he was lost while in search for his brothers (Gen. 37:16). He talked about his *devotion* to God before Potiphar's wife when she tempted him and he asked the Chief butler and baker in Prison why they were depressed, because he was concerned about their *disposition*.

> 'Dear brothers and sister, when troubles come your way, consider it an opportunity for great joy.'
>
> **James 1:2 (NLT)**

The Bible says we should see trouble as an opportunity for great joy. The right attitude for adversity is to be positive and optimistic. The right attitude is to keep believing your revelation not your situation. Most people are too negative to be successful. They are too pessimistic and love to attract the sympathy of others to themselves. But if Joseph was too negative and gloomy he would never had noticed the disposition of the chief butler and baker. Consequently, he would have died in prison. This is how wrong attitude stifles the destiny of great people.

Friends, no one is a success over night, they are only processed over time. You cannot pray, fast, cast or bind trials away. Sowing seeds is not an escape route to success either. You just have to go through the process to breakthrough with the promise. The key is to stay positive because crises are not always a sign of wrong decisions you may have made. They also signal your entrance into a new season.

> 'For <u>our present troubles are small and won't last long</u>. Yet they produce for us a glory that vastly outweighs them and will last forever.'
>
> **2 Cor. 4: 17(NLT)**

PONDER POINTS

1. Those who see the ultimate cannot be intimidated by the immediate.

2. The miracle you are believing God for may be hidden in the crises you're currently dealing with when you learn to see trouble as an opportunity.

3. Most times God will do some things *in* you, before he can do some things *for* you.

4. Sometimes the issues we face in life are divine indicators from God signaling that we are at the verge a major breakthrough.

5. Do not define yourself based on what you are going through. Define yourself based on your dream and where you are going to.

6. Challenges do not mean you are not in the will of God. Most times it means you are ready to come into the fullness of your destiny.

Situations Are Meant To Refine You, Not Define You

9

GREAT PEOPLE ARE REAL PEOPLE; THEY NEVER HIDE THEIR TRUE PERSONALITY BEHIND THEIR POSITIONS

The world is in dire need of real heroes and mentors that show us how they conquered and overcame the boisterous storms of life. Not shooting stars and short-lived celebrities that only reveal the superficial luster of fame for a while. But are too intimidated to display their real personality and the scars of failures they went through to become what they are today.

The easiest way to positively influence people is to be real. Not just by narrating the account of your achievement and counting the laurels of your accomplishments, but also telling people where and why you fell and failed. Great people have the audacity to be real; they never hide their real personality in the mask of their positions or situations. They are not polluted by success or diluted by failures; they simply know who they are, no matter where they are.

'... When only the brothers were left with Joseph, he told them who he was. <u>Joseph cried so loudly</u> that the Egyptians heard him and the people in the King's palace heard about it. He said to his brothers, "I am Joseph... I am your brother Joseph..."

Genesis 45: 1-4(NCV)

When Joseph met his brothers in Egypt, he was real with them. He told them who he was. He said, *'I am Joseph'*. He did not mask himself in fame and fortune. He didn't allow the veneer of pomposity, pomp or pageantry shroud the true essence of his personality. Hence, he was not ashamed to cry before them. How many people today in Joseph's shoes will do what he did? Joseph had opportunity to repay them for their evil deeds, yet he chose not only to forgive them but to be open and frank with them.

For me those words, *I am your brother Joseph* are loaded. Even though his brothers felt guilty about what they had done, I don't believe that was the reason he told them who he was. I believe Joseph wanted them to know that his position did not change him. He wanted to be open with them. No matter where he was and what he had attained, he wanted them to know that he was still Joseph, their brother. His position was not the source of his identity. He had a good self image and was comfortable to remove his mask of royalty.

Many people have hidden who they are in what they do or where they are, because it is the easiest thing to do. Anyone can recline comfortably in the seat of prominence and relax in a position of influence and affluence. But only few have the boldness to tell other people, this is who I am. Friends, we should learn from Joseph to be real.

It is better to be the testimony, than tell a testimony. People are inspired by examples and authenticity. You might be the Prince of Egypt now, but don't forget where you came from. Do not forget that you are still like every other person, susceptible to feelings, pains and issues.

How many people at the zenith of their profession and vocation today can say like Joseph, this is who I am without feeling vulnerable? How many can say, I am Joseph. I am still your brother; popularity did not change my personality.

A Suspect For Success: Setback For A Season, Setup For A Reason

We have seen seemingly influential people become nine day wonders. Like a candle in the wind, their transient stroll into the corridors of power seem to be forgotten so soon. All because they did not have the courage to say like Joseph, this is who I am. This is the real me; I am Joseph. Friends, people never really hang around pretentious people for a long time because they are phony and deceptive. The outer coat of pretense can only sustain you for a short while, but will never really make you a successful.

Significance and real success is not about intimidating people with position, status or titles. It is about contributing to the lives of others by giving them an opportunity to learn from your mistakes and misfortunes. It is about showing them the real you. Even God describes himself as *I am that I am*; a derivation of his personality, (Exodus 3:14). Besides, remember Jesus washed his disciples' feet and was crucified almost naked with out-stretched hands. He was genuine, open and sincere.

TAKE THE MASK OFF

The greatest prisoners today are not the convicts we see in any derelict penitentiary or dilapidated prison. They are those who have become experts at concealing their struggles and situations in life. The easiest way the enemy destroys people is by keeping them bound up with secret issues and toxic habits so that they are malignantly ravaged from within.

People who fall prey to this are always manipulative to others, intimidated by others and insecure with others. Even when they taste the fruits of success, they are too scared that any knowledge of their past would ruin their reputation and chances of further success. Hence, they appear sophisticated and posh on the outside, yet they are prisoners to their own success.

Professional actors and actresses are no longer in Hollywood but within us. We have all learned how to comfortably wear masks to cover our factual issues and identity. Don't let the enemy fool you, you are not the only one with a situation. [1]

In an interview about her book, 'The Crossings', Mrs. Serita Jakes captures this theme beautifully. She said, "We all have our closets, our skeletons. We all have things in our past that scare us... I've learned to embrace my own scars and share them as needed, particularly with the younger generation so they can understand I did not get to this place without trials, tribulation, scars and struggles to overcome....Through our scars and our stars, we need to become living letters that men can read every day. Those who are called have to become more humble, more transparent instead of covering and hiding. I want people to overcome fear. The fear of rejection, the fear of acceptance, and embrace the fact that the only being that knows all about us and loves us still is the Lord".[2]

Most of the people God used in the past that we refer to as great today were not necessarily perfect; they all had issues just like everyone. Yet they learned to lean on God's grace. Abraham lied about his wife being his sister. David committed adultery and murder. Paul slaughtered Christians. The list is endless.

Yet these people didn't allow personal issues, past accomplishments, present successes or public image to drive them to a point where they hid their need for internal healing and help. This is very crucial because most people drown in the sea of their own success. Their inflated egocentric image and exaggerated feeling of importance makes them too self-conscious to seek for solutions in times of distress.

WHERE ARE YOU HIDING?

I am reminded of the story of the first man, Adam. The first question God asked him was to assess his location and not his situation. He asked Adam *where are you,* not what have you done? (Genesis 3:9-10). But Adam was hiding in fig leaves.

Most people do not see a solution in what they are going through because they are blinded by their situation or their position. Like Adam, many are hiding in fig leaves because of past issues or present predicaments. They may smile publicly yet sigh privately. They may lead openly yet bleed secretly because they cover up secret issues and severe struggles. God is calling you; where are you? It's time to be real. I once read a powerful quote from an unknown source that said, 'Forget what you heard, recognize what you see. I know you heard the rumors... now here's the real me.'[3]

It takes a great man to be a real man. A real man that understands that greatness is not a measure of human perfection but a realization of human limitation that drives one to seek the grace and mercy of the Almighty God.

A great man is not a man without faults, flaws or frailties. But a man who has the humility to realize, admit, learn and teach others from his mistakes. Hence, we are great not because we are perfect, but because we lean on a perfect God. This attitude makes it easy to be real with people, no matter the height of greatness we ascend to.

What are you hiding in today? Like Joseph, it's time to take the masks off and be real. The desire to be like others and please everyone is the password to failure. Regardless of past difficulties or present adversities, you have to embrace your personality and accept your peculiarity. When we try to duplicate people's lives we may lose our originality. Our originality is in our difference. Our difference makes us valuable. When we are real, we can be examples that champion significant changes in people's lives.

I am often amazed at how God uses real broken people to reach the heartbroken. Recently, I attended a Joyce Meyer Conference and was surprised to know that this global ministry we celebrate was painted on the backdrop of a young girl that was sexually abused by her father at least 200 times before she was 18.[4] Nevertheless, Joyce Meyer chose to be real. By being real with people and sharing how she overcame her past it became a message, not bondage.

Friends, your worth was determined before your birth. God made you like Him. Any event that came after your birth is too late to determine your worth. You are already important; do not try to be. When you try to be what you are not, you lose who you are. Don't allow positions or situations to mask your real personality. Apostle Paul says we are the living epistles read by men (2 Cor. 3:2). Receive God's undeserved grace and use your life to help others.

PONDER POINTS

1. The world is in dire need of heroes that show us how they overcame the boisterous storms of life. Not short-lived celebrities that are too intimidated to show the scars of failure they went through to become what they are today.

2. A great man is not a man without faults, flaws or frailties, but a man who has the humility to realize, admit, learn and teach others from his mistakes.

3. The desire to be like others and please everyone is the password to failure.

4. Significance and success is not about intimidating people with positions and titles but giving them an opportunity to learn from your mistakes and misfortunes.

5. God uses broken people to reach the heartbroken because they are not polluted by success or diluted by failures. They know who they are, no matter where they are.

6. Greatness is not a measure of human perfection but a realization of human limitation that drives one to seek the grace and mercy of the Almighty God.

Great People Are Real People

10

THE MANIFESTATION OF YOUR DREAMS BEGINS WITH THE INTERPRETATION OF THE DREAMS OF OTHERS

Only those who live beyond themselves experience true success and satisfaction in life. These are those who strive to move beyond the shores of personal accomplishments to significantly impact others. Often times, those obsessed with the idea of their own personal fame or consumed with fantasies of status never reach their goals and full potential, because they just want to make a name for themselves.

The paradox of greatness is that we never experience lasting success only when we simply try to make ourselves successful but when we try to make others successful too. The validity and authenticity of your dream is not predicated on what it will make you but what it will make out of others; how it will impact people positively. While this might sound absurd because we live in a society that is driven by class, cash and celebrity status, the real way to succeed is by becoming a solution to others.

Joseph had a dream as a young boy, but his dream never came to fruition till he interpreted other people's dreams. When he was thrown into the prison, he had to interpret the dreams of the chief butler and baker, and eventually Pharaoh's dreams.

Most people with great dreams never see great open doors because they are too consumed with the fact that their dreams have not come to pass yet. They fail to realize that God always uses other people's situations to unlock their own breakthrough.

> *'And they (Chief Butler and Baker) said unto him (Joseph), We have dreamed a dream, and there is no interpreter of it. And Joseph said unto them, Do not interpretations belong to God? tell me them, I pray you.'*
> **Genesis 40: 8**

Imagine Joseph in prison. He had not yet seen the manifestation of his dream even though he was interpreting other people's dreams. To worsen matters, Joseph did not just interpret the chief bulter's dream, but had to watch him leave the prison back to the palace a few days later (Gen. 40:20-21). I wonder how Joseph felt watching someone who once sat with him leave him behind.

How many people today with unrealized dreams and incubating visions have the strength to readily offer assistance to others, especially when their help could be a major factor to the manifestation of the other person's dream? How many people would dare to be great and selfless by becoming a solution for someone else, even when they are still in a worse situation themselves? How many people would do what Joseph did? A great man is not only known by what he does when he is already known, but by what he does when he is not yet known.

The problem with most people today is not that they have a problem, but that they have failed to recognize the problems other people have. Problems are the hinges that swing the door of divine opportunities open for us. The same way we appreciate God for people's help when we are in dire need, we must also learn to also appreciate God when we are in a position to help other people. The answer to your prayers may just be a problem away.

You do not have to be in relief to offer someone else relief. Everything does not have to be perfect in your life before you help people. Often times it is our selfless service that gives birth to our breakthroughs. David showed up at the battle field with lunch in his hands for his brothers and ended up on the throne. Ruth found her husband Boaz through service. Abraham looked beyond his barrenness and offered to feed strangers who ended up being angels that prophesied about him having a son. It seems like God always unlocks the dreams of those that are concerned about others and not just themselves only.

When we reach the world through the eyes of her needs, we invariably build a memorial that would last forever.

Apostle Emma Okorie

WHOSE DREAM ARE YOU INTERPRETING?

My wife and I decided that a minimum of 20% of the proceeds from each of this book sold will go to missions, community development and charity work. Matt. 25:32-46(NCV) says, *'I was hungry and you gave me food... I was sick, and you cared for me.'* Notice that, although divine healing is very important, Jesus didn't say, I was sick and you healed me, but that you **cared** for me. This is really noteworthy.

God is very concerned about how concerned we are about people's needs. Whose life are you making better today? Whose dream are you interpreting? Little acts of affection speak louder than great words of consolation. No matter your state, strive to be a blessing today.

Your Manifestation Begins With The Interpretation Of People's Dreams

Relevance is the key for dominion in these last days. The world is waiting for the manifestation of the sons of God but how can we manifest if we are not relevant? We are called to be salt and light to the earth. Please notice that Pharaoh did not send for Joseph because he (Joseph) had a dream but because he (Pharaoh) had a dream. In fact, Pharaoh did not even know that Joseph had a dream, he was not concerned about all that. All he (Pharaoh) wanted was an interpretation of his own dream. Little did he know that the interpretation of his dream would lead to the manifestation of Joseph's dream too.

> 'And Pharaoh said unto Joseph, I have dreamed a dream, and there is none that can interpret it... And Pharaoh said unto Joseph, Forasmuch as God hath shewed thee all this, there is none so discreet and wise as thou art: ... And Pharaoh said unto Joseph, See, I have set thee over all the land of Egypt.'
> **Genesis 41: 15, 39, 41**

Your destiny is tied to people. Your dream is activated by people. Your vision is not about you but about other people. You are just a channel used to fulfill a divine agenda. Besides, God never uses and dumps anyone.

The rewards of success and prosperity are exclusively reserved rights of those who are committed to proffering solutions for people today. Those who go after material success always miss it, but those who go after relevance and impact will always dominate and leave a lasting legacy. The manifestation of your dream begins with the interpretation of other people's dreams. Whose dream are you interpreting? Whose lives are you making better? What memorial are you building in people's lives?

Success in life is all about helping people and by so doing, you are helping yourself.

Dr. Jude Ehiemere

We often pray for God's anointing and blessing in our lives, but what we fail to understand is that we have already been blessed and anointed for greatness. Consequently, God places us in adverse situations to reveal what He has deposited in our spirit. Otherwise how would we know what we have on our inside?

The problems we face are platforms of expression for the graces and gifts we have. They are indications that we have what it takes to be a solution because Like Joseph, God will not allow us to be in prison, if we did not have the capacity to interpret the dream of the prisoners. You are where you are not to complain or adjust to the negative climate, but to change it.

It is time to live beyond ourselves. I once heard a preacher say that we should endeavor to be *people millionaires* that influence millions of people positively, not just *paper millionaires* that want to make money only. [1] It is time to be a solution to local and global situations. We should strive to be the seed that meets the needs of others. My wonderful mother, Mrs. Esther Ehiemere, taught me that when I make other people's dream work, God will cause mine to work out. Friends, it's time to become relevant today. We are blessed to be a blessing to others. You can't put others first and be the last.

PONDER POINTS

1. The validity and authenticity of your dream is not predicated on what it will make you but what it will make other people.

2. A great man is not only known by what he does when he is already known, but by what he does when he is not yet known.

3. God always unlocks the dreams of those that are concerned about others and not themselves only.

4. The problem with most people today is not that they have a problem, but that they have failed to recognize the problems other people have.

5. Problems are the hinges that swing the door of divine opportunities open for us. You do not have to be in relief to offer someone else relief.

6. The rewards of success and prosperity are exclusively reserved rights of those who are committed to proffering solutions for people today.

11

IT'S COMEBACK TIME, YOUR SETBACK CANNOT STOP YOUR SET TIME

A couple of years ago I felt like nothing in my life was working. It seemed as if I was stuck in a particular spot and all my friends had moved on. The future just looked black and bleak. I fell to my knees in prayer to the Lord and He said to me, *'Waiting time is not wasted time. Just because you came later doesn't mean you are late, it only means you're the latest.'* I was encouraged by those words. It was like a ray of light in a dark lonely tunnel. Nonetheless, I initially only understood the first part of the sentence about the *waiting time*, but needed more clarity about *being the latest*. So I went back to God. He explained it to me and I am going to try to explain it to you because it revolutionized my thinking.

Many of us are familiar with Apple® products so I'm going to use them to buttress my point. The iPhone™ 3G was released in the summer of 2008. At that time, it was the best thing that happened to the telecommunications industry and everyone was crazy about it. More than three years later, the iPhone™ 4S was released in October of 2011.[1] There was a mad rush and people were eager and willing to queue all day just to get it because it was the hottest product in the market.

Remember that there was a three year difference in the release date of the iPhone™ 3G and iPhone™ 4S. But we never say that the iPhone™ 4S came late, we simply say it is the latest. The three years gap did not make it late; it just made it the latest. It only created more suspense and anticipation in people's minds. So just because the iPhone™ 4S came later than the iPhone™ 3G does not mean it came late, it just means it is the latest. It is all part of the market strategy.

Similarly, what we call lateness or delay is only our failure and misunderstanding of God's timing and dealing with us. It's part of God's strategy. It is part of His divine plan. He keeps you away from the public not to delay your manifestation, but to prepare you for greatness and heighten the expectation of people.

There were a lot of rumors and speculations before the iPhone 4S™ was released. I would say it was a suspect for success in the telecommunications industry. Even though people had not seen it, they suspected that it would have better functionality and performance than the previous models.

This is how God deals with us. He prepares a table for us in the presence of our enemies before inviting us. Perhaps you've been waiting on God to show up in your life. He just might be preparing your table, and He'll soon call you in. The bible says, In His time, He makes all things beautiful (Ecl. 3:11).

God is never late. He does not set His watch according to our clocks. He does not mark His dates with our calendar. Men may say since you came later, you will always be last and late. But God knows how to change breaking news into breakthrough news. After all, He created time from the matrix of eternity, so he knows when the time is right. David understood this and said in Psalms 31: 15(ESV) *'My times are in your hand...'*

WAITING IS NOT WASTING

Truth be told, one of the most difficult things to do in life is to just wait, especially when you have a burning dream and desire. But it always pays to wait for God's signal. If you are not patient, no matter how powerful your dream is, you may be the first casualty. Remember, they that wait upon the Lord renew their strength (Ish. 40:31).

No matter how you feel, you are not wasting if you are waiting on God's timing. You are actually growing and learning. Growing through the dark and learning through the pain. Some people argue that God is waiting on us to act, and I agree with this because sometimes He is. But I still believe that in some cases we have to wait on God. We have to wait for His timing. It is better to wait on God, than for God to wait on us to do what he has told us to do. The former is patience, the later is procrastination. Never confuse the two.

'... all the days of my appointed time <u>will I wait, till my change come</u>.'

Job 14:14

A miracle is not only when God does something *for* you, but when He does something *in* you. God working *in* you usually takes more time than Him working *for* you. God working in you is the process, but God working for you means favor and miracles. Premature exposure to the rays of success may cause us to miss crucial stages of growth and development that enable us to remain where our dreams have taken us to.

Maturity is a miracle inter-woven with time. Many people called Elizabeth barren, but she was not actually barren, (Luke 1:13). She was simply preserved for a particular time and for a higher calling. She was waiting, she was not wasting. God was preparing her for her set time. If she had gotten pregnant when people thought she ought to, John the Baptist would have missed the prophetic calendar and destiny of Jesus as a fore runner.

> 'For <u>ye have need of patience</u>, that, after ye have done the will of God, ye might receive the promise.'

Hebrews 10:36

Patience is a prerequisite in our destiny. The Bible says we need it to receive the promise. Joseph was seemingly forgotten in prison, but when the perfect time came, God brought him out to save the nations from famine and preserve a generation from scarcity, starvation and shortage. Nevertheless, he had to wait in prison till his set time.

Have you ever wondered how frustrating Joseph would have felt having a big dream but still living in a small prison? Have you ever pondered how the excitement of teenage dreams can precipitate leaving only the irritation of life's paradoxical predicaments as the days turn into weeks and the weeks turn into years? Or maybe you do not have to because you are presently wearing those shoes, and have resigned your dreams to fate because you feel forgotten, ignored and neglected. I want you to know, you are not alone. God is a very present help in trouble (Psl. 46:1). You may feel like you are in a setback now, but it's only a divine set up.

SETBACK ON PURPOSE

The word *setback* is a combination of two words, *set* and *back*. The word *set* means something that is programmed for a reason and prepared with a purpose. The word *back* means behind or reverse. Thus, a *setback* literally means a programmed backwards movement that is for a particular reason and a prepared purpose.

This means that even though we may feel like we accidentally found ourselves in a misfortune, misery or mistake, God still says your times are in my hands. It might be a unanticipated movement in an opposing direction but God knows how to bring it all together for a reason.

I once saw an archer many years ago using his bowstring and arrow to hit a target. I realized that in order for him to get a good shot at his target, he had to place the arrow on the string first. Then he pulled the string and arrow backwards before releasing the arrow forward towards its target.

> '*Children born to a young man are like arrows in a warrior's hands.*'
> **Psalm 127:4 (NLT)**

We are like arrows in God's hands. Many people today are in a setback. They are pulled back by the vicissitudes of life. But I want you to know that God, the master Warrior and Archer is still in control of the bow. You may see it as a setback in the wrong direction, but it is divinely programmed and planned for a target.

God will permit that setback only to allow you to gather enough momentum to face the future. That setback, whether it is in your family, relationship, career, business, health, or ministry, will not exterminate you but will empower you. The prison did not kill Joseph, neither will yours. The tomb could not hold Jesus, neither will yours. The lion's den could not kill Daniel, neither will yours. Whatever you're facing is all part of the plan to take you to the next level.

> 'Thou shalt arise, and have mercy upon Zion: for the time to favour her, yes, <u>the set time, is come.</u>'
>
> **Psalm 102: 13 (Webster)**

When your set time comes, God will do everything to get you to the top. He gave Pharaoh a dream that only Joseph had the interpretation to. God can create a situation that you only have the solution to. He'll organize crises just to promote, project and propel you. The king's heart is in God's hands and He turns it wherever He wills (Pro. 21:1).

> 'And it came to pass at the end of two full years, that Pharaoh dreamed… Then Pharaoh sent and called Joseph, and they brought him hastily out of the dungeon… And Pharaoh said unto Joseph, I have dreamed a dream… <u>And Pharaoh said unto Joseph, See, I have set thee over all the land of Egypt.</u>'
>
> **Genesis 41:1, 14, 15, 41 (ASV)**

YOUR RISING WILL BE SURPRISING

Imagine how Potiphar would have felt to see Joseph as prime minister after imprisoning him unjustly years back. Imagine how Joseph's brothers would have felt seeing him as prime minister after throwing him into the pit and selling him off to foreigners in a strange land. They must have been shocked and surprised. Friends, men might have said you are cast down, but God is saying it's your time for lifting. This is the dispensation for your manifestation; this is your set time. Get ready! Your rising will be surprising. Your testimony will amaze people.

> *'When men are cast down, then thou shalt say, <u>There is lifting up</u>…'*
>
> **Job 22:29**

One of the reasons why I chose Joseph as the main character of this book is because of the treasures we can glean from his experiences and the close similarity of his life to the life of Jesus. Both were loved by their father but hated by their brothers. Both were sold for money by the ones they trusted and loved.

Joseph went down to the pit; Jesus went down to hell to liberate those in bondage. Joseph was thrown into prison with two of the kings' servants and Jesus was crucified in-between two thieves. Both had their cloths torn and taken away from them; Joseph by his brothers and Potiphar's wife and Jesus by the soldiers. Both had to go through setbacks to have a comeback and eventually came into the fullness of their destiny at the age of 30. It was their release date, their set time.

> *A setback is a setup for a comeback.* [2]
>
> **Wiley Jolly**

These two characters are the perfect pictures of not just suspects, but prospects for success. From the onset of their lives, the potential, outlook and future of their dreams looked so radiant that it sparked fierce envy and vehement bitterness from people. Joseph's brothers wanted to kill him and King Herod wanted to kill Jesus too.

It is amazing how critical people can see the greatness you carry even before you even start feeling like you are great. Most people today are suspects for success and they do not even know. People around them have peered into their future and perceived the fresh smell of imminent greatness that lies ahead. They may try to sabotage your success or undermine our efforts, but they cannot kill the dream within. It is still alive. It is protected and preserved by God's grace for such a time as this.

Someone reading this book is a suspect for success too. Even though your dream has not materialized, you know deep down that you are destined for greatness. You may not even feel like one because of what you've been through, but you still are. You are destined for success.

I have good news for you, it is come back time. Your waiting time was not wasted time. You are a survivor because you held on. What should have killed you, healed you. What depressed others empowered you. You went through protracted storms and setbacks that brought down other people but you still chose to believe God.

As previously mentioned in the introduction, you are a threat to the enemy. All the attention may not be on you now, and like Joseph, you might be in the pit or prison. But the enemy knows that there is something about you. He can sense the great future God has prepared for you and he is trying to kill your spirit, steal your joy and destroy your soul. However, through it all you are still stronger, wiser and better. This is proof that God is up to something in your life. You are a suspect for success.

Did you notice that every time Joseph's clothes were forcefully taken from him, he went into a decline? When his brothers, took his coat of many colors, the next place he found himself was in the pit (Gen. 37:23-24). When Potiphar's wife took his clothes while attempting to drag him to sleep with her, the next place Joseph found himself was in the prison (Gen. 39:12-20).

However, when the King sent for him, he decided this time around I'm not going to allow anyone to put on my clothes for me. Similar to when people decide to help you and suddenly, out of the blue, decide to withdraw their support. If people put clothes on you, then people can take it off you. Joseph decided this time around, I'll do it myself. He must have said, 'Enough is enough with the turbulent seasons of inconsistencies in my life, this season of blessing will be permanent.'

'The king sent for Joseph... He shaved, <u>changed his clothes</u>, and went to the king.'

Gen. 41:14(CEV)

I believe that the first day Joseph sat on the throne, it dawned on him that he had always been destined for greatness. He realized why the enemy fought him hard all along. More importantly, he understood that God was with him from the very start and was working behind the scenes. It dawned on him that he was setback for a season, but setup for a divine reason. No wonder he told his brothers not to feel bad about what they did to him because God was behind it.

Friends, it may not be obvious to you now, and you may not understand what is really happening in your life but God is behind whatever you are going through now. He knows how to work it out for your God. Joseph understood this concept. He said to his brothers;

> 'But don't feel badly, don't blame yourselves for selling me. <u>God was behind it. God sent me</u> here ahead of you to save lives.'

Genesis 45: 4 (MSG)

You might be setback but it's only for a season because like Joseph said, God is behind it. That setback is only a setup in disguise for a divine reason. It's about time for you to discover why you went through it. The night is over. Your set time has come. The King has sent for you and it's an emergency. It's time to shave yourself and put on your garment. Destiny beckons. Now you realize like Joseph, everything you went through was not really about you. It was about God fulfilling His dream in your life. It was about your future. It was about the greatness in you. It was all a divine set up, because you are a suspect for success. Get ready because your rising will be surprising. It's comeback time; your setback cannot stop your set time.

MANIFEST!

PONDER POINTS

1. Waiting time is not wasted time. Just because you came later doesn't mean you are late, it only means you're the latest.

2. It's better to wait on God, than for God to wait on us to do what He has told us to do. The former is patience, the later is procrastination.

3. Premature exposure to the rays of success may cause us to miss crucial stages of growth and development that enable us to remain where our dreams have taken us to.

4. What we call lateness or delay is only our failure and misunderstanding of God's timing and dealing with us. It's part of God's strategy.

5. God is never late because He doesn't set His watch according to our clock; neither does He mark His dates with our calendar.

6. When we learn to trust God though our storms, setbacks and struggles, he knows how to change breaking news into breakthrough news.

GET CONNECTED

Today we are bombarded daily with headlines of violence, job loss, terrorist attacks, natural disasters, diseases, corruption, economic crises, drugs, war, racism, biological weapons, global warming etc. The list is endless. However, in the midst of all these, we can still experience heaven on earth. We can still live the life we've dreamed of.

I have discovered that there are two categories of people that find it difficult to really live life to its fullest. The first category are those who allow failure to get into their heart. They are always weighed down by life's issues. These people personalize failure and make it a part of their present life. They are hostage to the painful situation they face and forever visit the mortuary of the past to embalm the dead issues of their lives.

The second category of people allow success get into their head. They are intoxicated with the rich wine of success brewed from the refinery of their own competence. They are puffed up by their own exploits and obsessed with their achievements. They forever show-off the trophies of their own abilities and are preoccupied with the egocentric dividends of their success.

We are not meant to be bound by problems or blinded by our possession, position and power. We are to live a life of purpose. But how can we live a life of purpose if we don't understand the God of purpose, who is love personified? Talking about love, many today are looking for love in all the wrong places. They are looking for love in unhealthy relationships, alcohol, drugs, sex, bribery, and other social vices. In the process, they may run into personal pain or public fame. But deep inside they still know there is more to life.

> *'I came so they can have real and eternal life, more and <u>better life than they ever dreamed of</u>.'*
>
> **John 10:10 (MSG)**

Friends, power, possessions and positions do not satisfy. Pain, problems and predicaments may intensify. But it is only Jesus that can give you a better life than you ever dreamed of. He loves you because of who He is, not because of who you are or what you've done. He wants to give an essence to your existence. He can give you a fresh start and a second wind. The first step to experiencing this life of love, fulfillment and wholeness is by saying this prayer below;

> **Lord Jesus**
> ***I believe you died for me***
> ***Forgive me of all my sins***
> ***Come into my heart and be my Lord and Personal Savior***
> ***Today marks a new beginning in my life***
> ***Old things are passed away***
> ***Thank you Jesus***
> ***Amen***

Congratulations! This is the best decision you ever made. I'd encourage you to join and get involved in a grace-based church and maintain a daily relationship with God. You are now the righteousness of God in Christ; a new creature and your past is over. You can now reign in life and live like a King. Welcome to the family of Success!

DONATIONS

Through strategic partnership for social transformation, 20 Percent of proceeds from this book go into missions, charities and non-profit organizations, some of which are;

LIWOCARE started 1989 as a prison ministry in Nigeria and was registered in 2002. It has grown today and its central programs pivot around drug addicts, teenage crisis, rehabilitation of ex-convicts and youth enlightenment. It also focuses on assisting widows, feeding street beggars and providing support for HIV/AIDS infected and affected. Its goal is to give destiny to the destitute.

Champions Community Center (C3) was established in 1997, as a safe haven for youths between the ages of 12-18 in the North Houston area. Although C3 is still a safe-haven for teens, it has grown to become a much more far reaching entity, serving to enrich the lives of children, teenagers and entire families in our surrounding communities. For more info visit, www.champcenter.org

Mission Africa started in 2002 and was incorporated in 2006. Its mission is to give children in the remote villages of Africa the opportunity for better lives. The focus areas are education, health and poverty alleviation. The model is "Changing lives, one child at a time, one village at a time and one country at a time. It's headquartered in Seattle. For more info visit, www.missionafrica.us

Adonia Mission International is located in Bangui, Central African Republic and is currently into spiritual discipleship programs, medical outreaches, revival education and poverty alleviation schemes.

SELECTED REFERENCES

Chapter 1

1. http://csep10.phys.utk.edu/astr162/lect/light/bohr.html
2. http://www.quoteland.com/author/Bruce-Barton-Quotes/2944/

Chapter 2

1. http://www.understandingforce.com/usesoffriction.html
2. Paul Adefarasin; Change your World: The Call to a Performing Generation(Nigeria, Rock Publishing, 2006)
3. http://www.biblestudy.org/bibleref/meaning-of-numbers-in-bible/17.html
4. http://en.wikipedia.org/wiki/Prime_number
5. Apostle Ron Carpenter Jr. on TBN broadcast; http://www.rwoc.org/tv-broadcast-schedule.aspx

Chapter 3

1. http://www.wtal.org/about.html
2. http://www.quoteland.com/author/Mary-Lou-Retton-Quotes/1360/

Chapter 4

1. http://www.bukville.com/?p=896
2. http://www.brainyquote.com/quotes/keywords/future.html
3. Twitted by @iAmNurisha on 6th Febuary, 2012, https://twitter.com/#!/iAmNurisha
4. Joel Osteen on TBN, http://www.joelosteen.com/Broadcast/Pages/ThisWeeksMessage.aspx
5. Twitted by @ drmikemurdock on 14th January, 2012, https://twitter.com/#!/drmikemurdock

Chapter 5

1. Dr. Victor Ehiemere; Pursing your Purpose: Getting Rid of a lot to fulfill purpose (USA, Excel! Resources, 2010)
2. http://www.goodreads.com/quotes/tag/harmony
3. http://thinkexist.com/quotes/ben_stein/

Chapter 6

1. https://www.jhm.org/Resources/OnlineProgramming
2. http://www.brainyquote.com/quotes/quotes/j/jamesantho107683.html
3. http://www.brainyquote.com/quotes/quotes/d/dwightlmo379867.html
4. Twitted by @iAmNurisha on 18th November, 2011, https://twitter.com/#!/iAmNurisha

Chapter 8

1. Rev. Henry Emmanuel; Great Grace (UK, Jesus Joy Publishing, 2011)
2. Dr. Kelechi Chukwuemeka; It won't happen Again; Moving from Situation to Restoration (USA, Global Transformation Network, 2008)

Chapter 9

1. Dr. Kelechi Chukwuemeka; It won't happen Again; Moving from Situation to Restoration (USA, Global Transformation Network, 2008)
2. http://www.thegrio.com/specials/living-forward/serita-jakes-thegrio-interview.php?print=5
3. http://www.searchquotes.com/quotes/about/Being_Real/3/
4. Joyce Meyer's Personal testimony, http://www.youtube.com/watch?v=aaIHJSYXVfM

Chapter 10

1. Shiloh Message from Bishop David Oyedepo, Winners Chapel.

Chapter 11

1. http://en.wikipedia.org/wiki/IPhone
2. Wiley Joley; A Setback is a Setup for a Comeback(USA, 1999; Quotable Quotes©)

For testimonies and bookings, write:
Global Relevance Enterprises
globalrelevance@gmail.com
+1(713)261-8550, +1(951)203-695

www.ingramcontent.com/pod-product-compliance
Lightning Source LLC
Chambersburg PA
CBHW060816050426
42449CB00008B/1690